Taking Root

Taking Root

Conversion Stories for Children

The Lord's Garden, Volume 1

by
Diana Kleyn

REFORMATION HERITAGE BOOKS
Grand Rapids, Michigan

© 2006 by Diana Kleyn

Published by
Reformation Heritage Books
2965 Leonard St., NE
Grand Rapids, MI 49525
616-977-0599 / Fax 616-285-3246
e-mail: orders@heritagebooks.org
website: www.heritagebooks.org

10 digit ISBN 1-60178-001-X
13 digit ISBN 978-1-60178-001-0

The Lord's Garden

The books in this series are collections of devotional stories written for children. The stories are based on true happenings, gleaned from a variety of sources, and rewritten for contemporary readers. Most are culled from books of the nineteenth century, including several by Richard Newton. Modern presentations of these stories were originally published in *The Banner of Sovereign Grace Truth* magazine, and are now arranged thematically for the purposes of these volumes. Each story accompanies a passage of Scripture, and is intended to illustrate that particular biblical truth. Some stories are shorter, some longer. However, all will capture the attention of children, and hopefully their hearts.

Contents

—1—
Taking Root

Thou hast brought a vine out of Egypt: thou hast cast out the heathen, and planted it. Thou preparedst room before it, and didst cause it to take deep root, and it filled the land.
—Psalm 80:8-9

Throughout the Bible, God gives pictures, illustrations, and stories in order to help us understand His mighty work of salvation. In this passage from the Psalms, Asaph compares Israel to a vine or a plant. He says that Israel was like a beautiful plant that covered the hills (verse 10). God had brought Israel out of the terrible slavery of Egypt and had driven out the enemies of Canaan. With God helping them by warring against the many heathen living in and around Canaan, Israel was able to occupy the new land. "Thou preparedst room before it" means that God cleared away the heathen so that Israel could enjoy the blessings of the Promised Land of Canaan.

Asaph explains that God "didst cause it to take deep root, and it filled the land" (verse 9). In order for a plant to grow big and strong, it needs to have a healthy root system. Think of the parable of the sower in the New Testament. Jesus told this story to illustrate what happens when good seed is planted in different kinds of soil. The seed that fell on stony ground soon died because it didn't have enough soil to take deep root. The little plants began to grow quickly, "but when the sun was up, they were scorched; and because they had no root, they withered away" (Matthew 13:6). Good roots are necessary for good plants.

The picture of the plant that Asaph paints for us in Psalm 80 teaches us about what it means to be converted, or born again. Have you ever helped your mom or dad transplant a bush or tree? For one reason or another, the location of the bush is not right, and a change must be made for the benefit of the plant. You carefully dig around the bush, making sure not to damage the roots. A new place is chosen and prepared. Maybe weeds, debris, and rocks are removed. Then the bush is planted in the new location where it can grow healthy and strong in the fresh, rich soil.

This picture of a plant taking root is used to teach us the idea of conversion. Just like the Israelites in Egypt, we are born into sin and slavery. That means we belong to the enemy of God, Satan. We cannot prosper under Satan's rule; we will die. That is why we must be brought under the loving care of the perfect Gardener, the Lord Jesus Christ. Using Asaph's illustration in Psalm 80, we can say that God will destroy the weeds before you; He will plant you in good soil; He will cause your roots to grow deep into the soil.

In this way, the stories in this book have to do with plants taking roots. They are not tales of actual flowers, leaves, and dirt, but they are about spiritual plants in the garden of the Lord. God's people are like plants that grow in His garden. When someone's heart is turned from himself and his sinful ways to faith in Jesus and devotion to God, it is like a plant that is taken from the deadly soil in Satan's kingdom and tenderly planted by God in His good soil. Then the plant starts to shoot out roots into the rich new soil so that it can live and take nourishment. There is no way for a plant to have life unless it takes root, and there is no way for a person to have spiritual life unless God turns him or her out of the way of death and into the way of life.

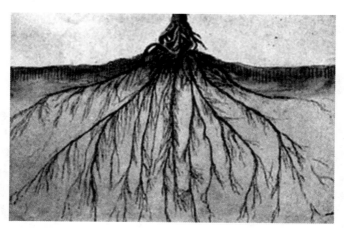

Jesus sacrificed His perfect life so that sinful people who are dead in their sins could have eternal life. So, as you read these stories, and even now as you think about the little picture God gives us in Psalm 80 of plants taking root, take the time to ask God about causing your heart to take deep root into the life-giving soil of Jesus.

—2—
A Little Girl's Sin Found Out

Take with you words, and turn to the LORD: say unto him,
Take away all iniquity, and receive us graciously: so will we
render the calves of our lips.

—Hosea 14:2

One Sunday, a minister preached from the text, "Be sure your sin will find you out" (Numbers 32:23). He said many solemn things about this earnest text. One of the things this minister said was, "If you do not find out your sin through the work of the Holy Spirit, and bring it to Jesus to get it pardoned and washed away through His blood, you may be sure that your sin will find you out, and bring you to the judgment seat of God. Then the Judge of heaven and earth will send you away into everlasting punishment."

In church that morning sat a little girl named Rachel. Before leaving for church that morning, Rachel had told her mother a lie. As she sat listening to the minister's words, she thought to herself, "Oh, that terrible lie! I must either bring it to Jesus, or it will find me out at the last day and bring me to punishment!" She became very anxious about her soul's salvation. She could not think of anything else. That night Rachel hardly slept. She tried to pray, but did not find any relief. Was God so angry with her that He would not hear her prayer?

The next morning, Rachel made up her mind to go to her minister, and talk with him about all she felt and feared. Rachel had to walk several miles in the rain to reach his home. She was warmly received by the pastor and his wife. Then Rachel poured out all her trouble. When she was finished, she said, "Oh, sir, what shall I do with my sin?"

"There is only one thing to do with it, my child," answered the minister, "and that is to lay it on 'the Lamb of God who taketh away the sin of the world'" (John 1:29b).

Then the minister knelt down with the little girl and asked the blessed Savior to forgive her sin, and comfort her wounded heart, and give her the help of His grace and Holy Spirit to keep her from sinning in this way any more.

Rachel went home feeling like a weight had been lifted from her heart. She thought about the text the minister had repeated to her several times before she left: "I acknowledged my sin unto thee, and mine iniquity have I not hid. I said, I will confess my transgression unto the LORD; and thou forgavest the iniquity of my sin" (Psalm 32:5). A love for the Lord Jesus began to bloom in her young heart.

—3—
The Pickpocket's Story

Let him that stole steal no more: but rather let him labor, working with his hands the thing which is good, that he may have to give to him that needeth. —Ephesians 4:28

At a meeting at the Bible Society once in London, a man spoke to the audience. "Gentlemen," he began, "I am happy there is such an excellent society such as this, which tries to raise money for Bibles. I thank God for the wonderful work you are doing. Listen for a moment to my story, and you will see that I have a good reason to thank God for the Bible.

"Several years ago," continued the man, "I belonged to a gang of pickpockets. One day, two of my friends and I were passing a church that was full of people. It was the anniversary of the Bible Society. Seeing so many people there, we thought it would be a good chance for us to get a lot of money by stealing it.

"The church was so crowded that my friends and I got separated from each other. I managed to get into the center aisle right near the front. The Ten Commandments, in large golden letters, were painted on the wall behind the pulpit. The first words that caught my eye were: 'Thou shalt not steal.' I stood rooted to the spot. I felt as if God Himself were speaking to me. My conscience troubled me so much that I began to weep right then and there.

"Meanwhile, my friends were trying to get my attention. It was time to get to work! But I forgot all

about them. I got out of the church as fast as I could, and moved to a part of the city where nobody knew me. I got a Bible, and for the first time in my life I began to read it. It showed me what a great sinner I was; but it also showed me what a great Savior Jesus is. I prayed to Jesus with all my heart. He heard my prayer, and now my sins are forgiven, and my soul is safe in Jesus.

"I am going to America, but before I go, I want to give a gift to the Bible Society. May God bless you in the great and wonderful work you are doing."

—4—
A Change of Heart

He hath shewed thee, O man, what is good; and what doth the LORD require of thee, but to do justly, and to love mercy, and to walk humbly with thy God?

—Micah 6:8

In 1673, Mr. John Flavel[1] was in London, visiting his friend, Mr. Boulter, a bookseller. Mr. Boulter told him this true story, to encourage him in his work of writing and preaching.

Some time before, a gentleman dressed in flashy clothes entered the shop. He had an air of arrogance and boredom about him which filled the godly bookseller's heart with pity. The stranger asked for books containing plays. Mr. Boulter told the man he did not have any, but showed him Mr. Flavel's little book entitled, *Keeping the Heart*. He urged the man to read it, telling him it would do him more good than reading plays. The gentleman read the title, and thumbed through the pages. Then he exclaimed, "You want me to buy this book? This author is a fanatic!"

Mr. Boulter shook his head. "No, he's not a fanatic. Read the book and you will find him to be

a very wise man. You have no right to make a judgment on this book when you haven't even read it,"
the shopkeeper reasoned.

At last, the man gave in and bought the little
book, but he told Mr. Boulter he would not read it.

"What are you going to do with it then, since you bought it?" asked Mr. Boulter.

"I will tear it up and burn it, and send it to the devil," the man replied roughly.

Mr. Boulter responded, "Well then, you should give it back if you are only going to destroy it."

"No, no, I will read it," promised the gentleman.

"If you do not like it after you've read it, you may bring it back and I will give you a full refund," the shopkeeper stated.

About a month later, the same gentleman came to the shop. He was no longer rough and rude, but serious and polite. Gone were the flashy clothes; instead he wore a plain but well-tailored blue suit. His demeanor was no longer proud and disinterested, but humble and sincere. "Sir, I most heartily thank you for putting this book into my hands. I bless God who moved you to do it; it has saved my soul. I will always be thankful that God led me into your shop!" Then he bought a hundred more of those books, and told Mr. Boulter, "These are for the poor, since they cannot come and buy them."

What a beautiful change of heart the Lord worked in this man's life! The Lord has no end of means of converting lost sinners to Himself. This man was not looking for salvation—he even despised Mr. Flavel's book at first. But God rescued this foolish man from destruction. Maybe you are not rude and disrespectful, but every person needs a new heart. Has your heart been renewed? Have you repented of your sins? Has the Lord Jesus washed away your sins? Look to Jesus for salvation, for He is the only Way. Read His Word, and speak to Him in prayer. He has promised that those who come to Him will never be cast out.

---

[1] **John Flavel** (c. 1628-1691), a Puritan preacher, was born at Bromsgrove, and studied at Oxford. His father, Richard Flavel, and his mother both died of the great Plague in 1665. He became the pastor at Dartmouth, but was sent away in the Great Ejection of 1662, continuing, however, to preach there secretly. His preaching was very effective and gladly received because of his simple, earnest messages. In those days of persecution and uncertainty, his cheerful encouragements were a blessing to God's people, and his solemn warnings were used by the Holy Spirit to save many souls.

—5—
Martha's Bible

And Jesus answered him, saying, It is written, That man shall not live by bread alone, but by every word of God.

—Luke 4:4

A young woman named Martha worked at a cotton mill in England many years ago. She was married to an alcoholic, who wasted their money on alcohol. All they could afford was a cold, damp basement apartment. Martha worked long hours to earn enough to pay the rent and buy the food. She tried to hide the money, but her husband, David, often found it.

One day, one of the women who worked at the mill asked Martha if she would like to buy a Bible. "You can own a Bible by paying just a little bit each week," the woman told her.

Martha said she would think about it. She knew they needed every penny Martha earned, because her husband, David, did not work. Making a bold decision, Martha decided to go ahead and buy the Bible. After all, she was the one that earned the money, and her mother had always told her it was important to read the Bible. Finally, after many weeks of work, Martha took home her beautiful new Bible. Proudly, she laid it on the table in her home. When Martha's husband came home from spending the evening with his friends, he noticed the new Bible on the table. Martha expected him to scold her for spending money on something that they didn't think was absolutely necessary. David, however, did not become angry. Instead, he seemed almost pleased. He picked it up and opened it.

"Martha, read this story to me," demanded David, who could not read or write. "I've heard people talk about the Bible, but never paid much attention before. I want to know what's in this Book."

So Martha read aloud, and her husband listened. She began at the place where David had opened the Bible—the story of Joseph. They became so interested, that they read the whole story before going to bed. The next day was Sunday, and since Martha did not have to work, and they had never gone to church before, they continued reading in the new Bible. They discovered what God says about sin, and what must happen to the sinner if he is not renewed. They began to ask, "Lord, what must we do to be saved?"

Their lives were changed. They went to church. David stopped drinking. They searched the Scriptures. And the Lord converted them both.

David started a new job. Do you know what it was? He sold Bibles! He visited fairs, races, and marketplaces for the purpose of selling Bibles. He prayed that many so-called "hopeless cases," such as he had been, would be rescued from eternal death through this means. In his lifetime, David sold about 30,000 Bibles and New Testaments. Who can tell the results which followed from the Bible Martha took home on that memorable Saturday night? Thirty thousand Bibles and New Testaments were sold because of David and Martha's conversions. The Lord can bless the simplest means. Ask the Lord to make you able and willing to serve Him.

—6—
"What Shall it Profit?"

For what shall it profit a man, if he shall gain the whole world, and lose his own soul? or what shall a man give in exchange for his soul?
                                                              —Mark 8:36, 37

"Andy Allen, you're not ready for church yet! Hurry, or we'll be late!" urged Clara as she entered the kitchen where her husband sat reading the newspaper. It was the newlyweds' first Sunday together in their new home. Andy had bought the home after

their engagement, choosing a beautiful two-story mansion set in perfectly landscaped gardens. He had hired the best interior designer he knew to furnish the house to welcome his new bride.

Clara had been raised by a kind great-uncle, who cared for her lovingly, surrounding her with all the comforts and luxuries he could afford. Her great-uncle Martin was a God-fearing man, and Clara seemed to take to heart his careful teachings.

When she became a young lady, however, handsome, fun-loving Andy Allen had won her heart. Uncle Martin had gravely asked her if Andy loved the Lord. Clara had looked away, only saying, "He promised to go to church with me."

"Marry only in the Lord, Clara," admonished her great-uncle.

These words now suddenly returned to her memory as she looked at her handsome young husband.

"Are you really going to church today in this cold weather?" he asked with a smile.

"I have never stayed home from church unless I was sick," countered Clara in surprise.

Andy only laughed and then cradled his head in his hands. "I think I'm getting a headache, Clara! Can't you stay home and read to me?"

Clara looked at him incredulously and replied, "You are not sick, Andy! I think it's wrong to stay home from church if you are healthy. Won't you come with me?"

"But where would we go, my dear wife?"

"Don't you have a church you attend here in your city?" Clara was beginning to worry. Was Andy not religious at all?

"The only church I have attended in the last ten years is your little brick church. I feel I have done my duty so well that I should be considered religious enough to last the rest of my days." He noticed her lip quiver and dropped his joking tone. "But don't look so sad, Clara. I will go anywhere to please you. I know of a beautiful church on Grand Avenue. We will go there, though I have no idea what it's like."

It was an elegant, stately church. The brilliant light which flowed through the stained glass windows almost dazzled the sight of the young woman, who was accustomed only to the plain colors of the humble village church. The voice of the deep-toned organ rolled through the marble hall and then burst forth into a lively tune unfamiliar to her ears. In spite of all its grandeur, however, God seemed somehow nearer in the little church at home, which nestled down among the grassy mounds and moss-grown headstones, seemingly always pointing to a life beyond this one.

When the minister arose, she noticed his graceful air, the polished words and sentences that flowed so smoothly from his lips as he read them from the page before him. But it all seemed so lifeless, so empty. Clara felt that her soul had not been fed, as they drove away from the marble church, but there were many new sights all around to distract this country girl in the city. Andy was glad to be finished with his duty of church attendance, and was quite pleased with himself for his act of self-denial.

When they reached home a message was waiting for them, inviting them to visit the fashionable Harveys. Their limousine would pick the Allens up at three that afternoon. Clara was not comfortable with the thought of ignoring the fact that it was the Sabbath. She knew that the Harveys were not religious.

Suddenly, Clara was filled with an overwhelming feeling of homesickness. How she would have loved to visit her dear great-uncle Martin, who would talk to her about the sermon he heard that morning! But he was far away, in another state. Tears filled her eyes. Andy saw, and was irritated.

"You know I went to church to please you this morning. I am sure you will be kind enough not to embarrass me by turning down the Harveys' invitation. I know they would be seriously offended if we don't go! They want to welcome you to the city and show you around."

Clara yielded to his logic, and with sad misgivings, prepared herself for the visit.

Mrs. Harvey was very courteous and pleasant. The conversation revolved around frivolous subjects, until in the excitement of the drive Clara almost forgot what day it was. When they approached the Harvey residence, Mrs. Harvey insisted that they have dinner together. The food was delicious and the company pleasant. Andy was a devoted husband, and took care not to ignore his new bride. Clara felt the Harveys were enjoying themselves as much as she was.

But underneath all her pleasure was a dull sense of pain and a consciousness of wrong-doing. When she reached home again, a flood of regretful sorrow swept over her, and she wept bitterly. Andy tried to soothe her grief, and secretly determined to rid Clara of the "superstition" which caused his dear wife so much unhappiness. He felt he would be doing her a favor to erase all the pious influences of her great-uncle which caused so much unnecessary guilt. "You have done nothing wrong, dear Clara," he said gently. "You have only spent a pleasant afternoon and evening with friends. We had to eat somewhere, and what difference does it make if it was at their house or ours? Life is meant to be enjoyed, and friends are a gift. Religion should make people happy. I am afraid yours has not made you happy today, Clara, so I don't think it's good for you. But if it makes you feel better, I'll go to church with you every Sunday morning."

It was a little comforting to hear Andy say he intended to go to church with her in the future, so Clara dried her eyes and smiled at her husband.

So the days and weeks continued. They were happy, but little by little, Clara's faith was worn away. Andy introduced his lovely wife to many worldly people, and slowly but surely, Clara became accustomed to living a worldly life.

Clara never fully gave up "religion," but the pious teachings of her Uncle Martin were watered down until there was not much substance left. Instead of the sure foundation which has Jesus Christ for its cornerstone, and a religion which teaches repentance, faith, humility, and self-denial, Clara embraced false teachings which proclaimed that in the end, everyone would be saved, and that there was good in everyone.

A writer Andy introduced to Clara became her favorite. All through this woman's writings ran a thread of truth, but it was bent out of shape by many falsehoods. Much was said about the love and mercy of God, but the fact that He is also a just God who by no means clears the guilty, was set aside as too harsh and distressing. "God is too kind and loving to send anyone to hell," said Clara's new friend. "He will save everyone eventually. We all take different paths, but they all lead to God in the end."

Time rolled on, and Clara and Andy were happy. They loved each other and life was pleasant. They had a little boy, Albert, who was the joy of their hearts. Life was grand, they thought.

~~~~~

The rain was dashing against the window panes one November night as an anxious group gathered in the little boy's nursery. They were standing on either side of a beautiful crib. There lay little Albert, tossing and turning, his little face flushed with fever. Clara wept as she wiped her son's face with a cool cloth.

"Do you think there is any hope he will recover, Doctor?" Andy whispered hoarsely. Clara looked up at the doctor with pleading eyes.

"He is in a very critical condition, sir," replied the doctor. "If I had been in town when he first became ill, I think the fever would not have gone so high. Everything depends on quick action. We must do what we can now to make up for lost hours."

But all the doctor's efforts proved useless. Albert lingered through the long night, and when morning dawned, he opened his eyes and looked at Clara.

"Mama!" whispered the little boy. He stretched out his arms to her. The parents smiled at each other in silent joy. Only the old physician looked grave and sorrowful. This little light was fast fading, and this was its dying flicker. Tenderly Clara held him in her arms. "Good-night, Mama and Papa," said Albert softly, "I'm going to sleep now."

It was over. Their little boy was dead. Clara and Andy could not be comforted. Their hopes and plans were dashed. Their wonderful life was suddenly interrupted by the reality of death and sorrow. Andy was crushed. He could not comfort his wife, so great was his own grief. He covered his face with his hands and sobbed as he had never done before.

Clara felt as though her heart were cold and dead. She could not cry. The pain was too great, too overwhelming. These mourning parents needed Someone to lean on, but they had no one.

Time, the great healer, wore away the sharpness of the loss of the child, but Clara could never again enjoy life as before. The parties and entertainments which had formerly seemed so pleasant no longer brought joy. A soft sadness rested on her heart, and she would wander about her house, looking at Albert's toys and pictures. Day by day she became weaker, and her health failed. Her cheeks were pale and shadows darkened her eyes. Her smiles were hollow and did not reach her eyes.

In her sorrow, she began to think of her dear Uncle Martin, who had died not long ago. She had not visited him once since she married Andy. A longing filled her heart; somehow she knew that he would have had words of real comfort during this awful time. Her long-neglected Bible was retrieved from a trunk in the attic, and she began to read it with a kind of desperation. The Bible had been her mother's, and along the margins were delicate pencil markings, pointing to precious promises. How eagerly Clara read them now! When she grew too tired to continue reading, she asked Andy to read to her. He did so because he loved her, but he could give her no spiritual advice. He gave her the best care he could, but could not care for her soul. He did not share her spiritual hunger.

Was there no one to offer a word of lasting truth? In His great mercy, God provided someone. Albert's nanny, Margaret, often came to visit. She had loved Albert, and she understood Clara's grief. But even better, Margaret loved the Lord, and she saw how much Clara needed Him. She prayed she would be able to bring God's Word to Clara's heart. She told Clara how much Albert had loved the Bible stories, especially the story of the Baby born in Bethlehem.

"Yes, I know," nodded Clara with a faint smile. "He used to talk about Jesus like He was real." The tears came again, and she reached for her handkerchief. "I remember Albert said something once about his sins, but I didn't want to hear about my little boy having any sins."

Margaret began to talk to Clara about "Baby

Jesus" who grew up to be the Savior sent by God the Father. Plainly and simply, Margaret pointed Clara to the Lamb of God as the only Savior, praying in her heart that the Holy Spirit would bring home the truth with power.

At length a little light dawned on Clara's mind. "I am like a wandering sheep, Margaret," she said thoughtfully. "Do you think He will receive even such a foolish wandering sheep as I am?"

"Absolutely!" assured Margaret. "He said, 'For the Son of man is come to seek and to save that which was lost'" (Luke 19:10).

Clara folded her hands tightly together and exclaimed, "Oh, then I will cast myself upon His mercy! Only His mercy can save me, for I can do nothing to make myself acceptable! Oh, all those wasted years!"

She leaned back in her chair and closed her eyes. A faint motion of her lips told of the silent prayer her heart was offering before the throne of grace. When she opened her eyes some time later, Margaret saw the beginnings of new hope shining in Clara's eyes. Margaret came to visit Clara often, and what wonderful visits they had! How Clara drank in the treasures of God's Word! How real was her sorrow over her wandering ways, but how deep was her love and thankfulness to the Savior for seeking and finding her! At last, she knew true joy.

Clara did not live many years longer. She died a

happy Christian. Her one great grief, however, was that her beloved husband was not interested in her new-found joy. He wanted nothing to do with the Bible. He did not want to turn to the God who had taken away his precious son. Till his dying day, Andy remained bitter, and refused to give his heart to God.

It is a dangerous step indeed for a young Christian to form a life-long union with one who is a stranger to God. "Be ye not unequally yoked together with unbelievers: for what fellowship hath righteousness with unrighteousness? and what communion hath light with darkness?" (2 Corinthians 6:14). This is a command which may not be lightly broken.

Children and young people, you must ask the Lord, first of all, for your own salvation, but you may also ask Him to choose a husband or a wife for you, one who also loves the Lord. "Love not the world, neither the things that are in the world. If any man love the world, the love of the Father is not in him. For all that is in the world, the lust of the flesh, and the lust of the eyes, and the pride of life, is not of the Father, but is of the world. And the world passeth away, and the lust thereof: but he that doeth the will of God abideth for ever" (1 John 2:15-17).

—7—
God's Word Satisfies

For he satisfieth the longing soul, and filleth the hungry soul with goodness.

—Psalm 107:9

Situated between the Russian Federation and China is the little country of Mongolia. This country has a long history. Since about the 13th century there was a group of people in this country called the Tartars, or Tatars. In the 19th century, two Tatar chiefs traveled to St. Petersburg in Russia to learn the Russian language and to study some of the arts and customs of the Europeans. This would be beneficial for them economically, that is, for trading goods and making money. These two chiefs brought with them letters from their tribes, stating that they were trustworthy, honorable men.

A German missionary, who was translating a part of the new Testament into the Tatar language, was delighted to meet these chiefs, and asked them to help him in his work. This immense task kept the three men busy for several months. They asked the missionary many questions about Jesus, the Savior, and the truths He taught.

At last came the day when the translation was

finished. The two chiefs sat in silence by the missionary as if they were not willing to leave him.

"Have you any questions to ask, my friends?"
inquired the missionary.

"None," was their answer.

"We wish to tell you that we believe the religion
of that Book," continued one of the chiefs, pointing
to the New Testament which lay on the table. "We
have lived in ignorance, and been led by blind
guides. We have read the books which tell about the
religion of the god Foh, who is worshiped in our
country. But the more we read those books, the less
we understood them, and the more empty our
hearts became. Your Book is very different from anything we ever heard before. The more we read the
words of God, the better we understand them. It
seems as if Jesus Himself were talking to us. Now we
know how to get our sins pardoned, and where to
find the help we need in trying to serve Him. That
Book satisfies our hearts and makes us feel happy."

What makes you happy? Are you happy? Do you
love the Bible? Read the Bible every day, and do not
neglect this live-giving Book! Pray for a blessing as
you read it.

—8—
A Mocking Discussion of the Bible

Wash you, make you clean; put away the evil of your doings from before mine eyes; cease to do evil.
—Isaiah 1:16

Years ago, when America was still a rough, young country, twelve young men set out from England to see this great new land. After a long ocean voyage, the men finally arrived. They worked hard during the summer, but soon winter forced them indoors. As time went on and the nights became long, the men grew bored. They were tired of playing one card game after another. There was nothing else to entertain them in this empty, wild country, so they tried to think of something to amuse themselves. Finally one of the men suggested that they have a mocking discussion of the Bible. Several of the men had tucked a Bible in their suitcases, at the insistence of their mothers, but until now, these Bibles had remained unread. Some of the men protested against the idea of a debate, but others thought it might be fun.

"We'll have to have some of us argue against it and some for it," stated Charlie. "John, you're good at talking. Which side do you pick?"

"But I don't know anything about the Bible!" protested John.

Charlie grinned at him. "Then we'll make you the defendant."

The other men laughed. This might prove to be fun after all! They chose Michael to argue against the Bible. His task was to try and bring out many

"contradictions," "faults," and "impossibilities" in God's Word.

At first the men didn't take it very seriously, but as the other ten egged them on each evening, the competition grew more intense. In order to try to win the debate, John began to study his Bible. At first, John studied only to try to win, but the more he studied, the more interested he became by the beauty, majesty, and wisdom of the Book. With each debate, the men could see that John believed the Word more and more fully. He was no longer a mocking, arrogant unbeliever. Joy and peace now reigned in his heart. His speeches about the Bible were heartfelt and persuasive. So great was the effect of his arguments and testimony that other men were brought to a knowledge of the truth as it is in Jesus. The result of this "mocking discussion of the Bible" was that all but one of the men were converted to God.

—9—
Shusco the Indian

Jesus answered and said unto him, If a man love me, he will keep my words: and my Father will love him, and we will come unto him, and make our abode with him.
—John 14:23

Shusco was an Ojibwa Indian. The date and place of his birth are unknown, but it is believed that he was born near Mackinac Island in Michigan. He was left an orphan when he was about ten days old. During his childhood he was shuffled between various caregivers among his Indian relatives. When he was about fifteen, he became a medicine man, or "mystery man" as he was sometimes called. He was thought to be able to cure diseases, bring rain to water the earth, and held a position of high regard among the Indians. But Shusco also became an alcoholic.

Shusco's wife, Sarah, went to hear some visiting missionaries one day, and the Lord converted her. The Savior was now precious to her soul, and she felt great concern for the soul of her husband. Shusco was deep in sin's grip, drinking and practicing his "medicine" among the people. He sincerely believed that he was doing good among his fellow Indians with his practices. Shusco's wife told him that he was deceiving the people and that his "medicine" was a sham. Of course, Shusco did not like to hear this, saying that he was happy with the religion of his forefathers and did not want the white man's religion.

Patiently, Sarah explained who the Great Spirit really is, and what is written in His Book. She told him about sin and the sinfulness of the human heart. She also told her husband about the Lord

Jesus Christ, the Way of Salvation. She told him that the Holy Spirit could make his heart better, and that anyone who died without the renewing grace of the Spirit would be forever miserable.

Shusco did not like his wife's words, but he could not forget them. When he thought of them, he was troubled. Finally, by God's grace, he decided to give up practicing his powers.

It was in the year 1828 that Shusco felt convinced he was a sinner, and for some time he was overwhelmed with a view of his past sins. His wife noticed that he was distressed and asked him what was wrong. He replied that he was sick at heart.

"You must pray to God," she said, "and He will forgive you."

"How can He forgive so great a sinner as I am? I have spent all my life in sinning against Him!" exclaimed Shusco.

"But," Sarah answered, "He will forgive you for the sake of Christ if you will pray to Him. He forgave me, so I know He will forgive you too."

Shusco tried to pray, but he could find no relief. His one great struggle was against his drinking. He earnestly desired to be delivered from this sin. One night he arose from his bed and went to pray. He cried out to God until he found his burden was gone. "The hard thing in my heart was taken away and I am not sick any more," he later said.

His heart was filled with love to God and to

others. Even nature seemed more beautiful than ever before: The sun shone brightly, the birds sang sweetly, nature shouted God's praises.

When Sarah saw him at breakfast that morning, she asked, "How do you feel now?"

"Very happy," replied Shusco. "My heart is not sick anymore, and I love God."

"It is the Lord's day today, Shusco," said Sarah. "We must not work today, but pray to God."

Shusco thought about the missionaries on the Island of Mackinac. Formerly, he had scorned them, but now he felt a desire to meet with them. "I want to tell them I love God now, and that I am very happy," he told Sarah.

The news of Shusco's conversion spread quickly. Everyone was amazed, and could hardly believe it at first, but his humility and love to Jesus were clear and there was no room for doubt. Shusco's lodge was no longer a place for drinking parties; now it was a place for prayer and praise.

One day, Shusco heard some news that made him anxious. He was told that some Indians were coming to visit. He had many fears, because formerly these Indian friends came in order to drink. Shusco spent much time alone in prayer in the days before their visit. He knew he would be tempted by things he formerly enjoyed.

When the Indians arrived, he greeted them in a friendly manner. Then, since it was his time for morning devotions, he went in the woods to pray. He was gone such a long time that his wife began to worry. Finally, he returned and explained that now he was ready to visit with the Indians. He found his Indian friends in one of the lodges. All of them were already drunk. They tried to get Shusco to drink along with them, but he refused.

"Why is it, Shusco, that you will not drink with us now, when you always used to? You loved to drink!" taunted the Indians.

"The Great Spirit has helped me to stop drinking," explained Shusco. "At first, I tried to stop in my own strength but I could not. Now I have God's strength in me, and I have no more desire for whiskey or other strong drink. I used to be unhappy, but now I am happy. My heart is clean."

Sunday was Shusco's favorite day of the week. He used to go to each one of the lodges in the village on Saturday evening to remind the people that the following day would be the Lord's Day, and that they must all go to the house of God.

Once, he was on a trip to another island to make sugar. He tried to keep track of the days of the week by making notches on a stick. But one day he forgot to make a notch. When the Lord's Day came, Shusco thought it was Saturday. So he ate his breakfast and went out to work. Someone noticed Shusco working, and was surprised. When he told Shusco that it was Sunday, he immediately dropped his tools, and went into the tent feeling very sad.

The following week, he visited the missionaries. He looked pale and frightened. "I am very sorry," he said as soon as he entered the mission house. "Perhaps you have heard what I have done."

"What have you done?" asked the missionaries kindly.

"I have broken the Sabbath day!" cried Shusco miserably. He explained what had happened. "I wanted to tell you myself before you heard it from someone else."

The missionaries prayed with him and read the Bible. Shusco returned home, knowing that God had forgiven him.

Shusco had a deep longing for others' salvation. He was so happy that the Lord had saved him, that he wanted others to enjoy the same grace. Often he would be seen visiting his friends and relatives, telling them about the riches of the Lord Jesus Christ.

A few weeks before his death, the family of his grandson came to visit him. None of this family knew the Lord. Every morning Shusco would visit with them and pray with them. Soon after their arrival, Shusco became lame and could not walk anymore, but he determined to use the time he had left on earth to tell his family about his precious Savior. He would creep to their lodge on his hands and knees in order to share the love of Christ with his beloved family.

On the morning before his death, his wife saw that he was very ill. She sat down beside him and wept.

"Do not weep, Sarah," said Shusco. "I am going to leave you, but God will take care of you. God has promised to take care of His children. Look to Him in prayer. He has promised that what we ask for in prayer in His name, He will give us. Remember what I say, for perhaps this is the last time I shall speak to you. Perhaps you also will soon come where I am going. Tomorrow, or the next day, perhaps I shall go."

Sarah went out to fetch some wood to stoke up the fire, and when she returned, he was committing his soul to his Savior, and Sarah to His fatherly care. Then his breathing stopped. He was calm and happy to the last hour of his life. He died on September 30, 1837.

Shusco loved the Lord Jesus Christ, and he was happy. Do you also love the Lord? Have your sins been washed away? Is it also your desire that your friends and family love the Lord? Do you pray for them?

—10—
Afraid to Go Home

Repent ye: for the kingdom of heaven is at hand.
—Matthew 3:2

During the mid 1800s, many towns and villages in America experienced the blessings of revival. In one particular congregation, a twelve-year-old boy approached one of the elders after a service. He was greatly distressed, and asked the elder for help. The elder asked him what made him feel so distressed.

"My sins, sir!" exclaimed the boy. "I am a great sinner in God's sight, and I'm on my way to hell! What must I do?" He wrung his hands as tears coursed down his flushed cheeks.

The elder laid a gentle hand on the boy's shoulder. "You must go home and read the Bible, and pray to God to give you a new heart," he advised.

The boy looked up at the elder with alarm in his serious brown eyes. "Sir, I am afraid that if I wait to get home, I may die on the way, and then it will be too late!"

Sympathy and shame filled the elder's heart, and tears sprang to his eyes. He felt reproved by the boy's earnestness. He had a better solution, one he should

have given first of all. "Dear child, if you are afraid
to go home because you may die in your sins, then
you must repent right now and believe in Jesus
Christ. When the prison guard asked Paul and Silas,
'What must I do to be saved?' they answered,
'Believe on the Lord Jesus Christ, and thou shalt be
saved' (Acts 16:30, 31). Let's pray right now. Before
you go home, you must submit yourself into His gracious hands."

Together they knelt, both shedding tears. Both
prayed, the boy begging God for forgiveness, the
elder reminding God of His own promises to
repenting sinners. Tears of sorrow turned to tears of
joy, and the boy went home rejoicing in his new-
found Savior.

Children, are you ever troubled by your sin? Have
you ever felt afraid to die, like the boy in this story?
Turn, right now, to Jesus and ask Him to cleanse you
and forgive all your sin. "If we confess our sins, he is
faithful and just to forgive us our sins, and to cleanse
us from all unrighteousness" (1 John 1:9).

—11—
The Gift

Thanks be to God for his unspeakable gift.
—2 Corinthians 9:15

"I know I'm going to win a prize," Edward told his friends. "I studied very hard for this exam."

Nervous-looking students filled the classroom. Today was the big day when Mr. Howard would test his history students. His exams were rumored to be very difficult. Some students, like Edward, had studied hard, and felt prepared. Others, however, had not bothered to study, thinking they would never be able to pass such a difficult exam no matter how hard they studied.

In the front of the classroom was a long table covered with books. Some books were big and expensive-looking, while others were paperbacks of various sizes. There were Bibles and small New Testaments, and books about different time periods in history. These were the prizes. The better the students did on their exam, the better their prize would be. The students looked at the books on the table, asking each other which book they were hoping to receive.

Edward noticed one book in particular. It was a

beautiful book about Roman history. Edward loved this period in history, and had read many books about it. He would love to own this book! Then he could read it as often as he wished, and study the detailed drawings in its pages. He set his heart on getting that prize. Several times during the exam, his attention wandered to the book on the table, and he had to remind himself to do his work well or he would never win the prize.

The following week, Mr. Howard handed back the exams. Edward had done very well: he had gotten the highest grade in the class, together with another boy named John. He was thrilled! Now he was certain he would get the best prize—the book about Roman history! But instead of receiving the book he had set his heart on, the teacher smilingly presented him with a beautiful Bible. It was black with gold letters on it. Instead of being thankful, however, Edward's eyes filled with tears as he watched the teacher present the book about Roman history to the boy who had achieved the same grade as Edward. He would have loved to trade with him, but had sense enough to realize that would be rude.

Edward's parents sympathized with him. They did not understand why Mr. Howard thought a Bible was a more valuable prize than the book their son wanted. They told Edward they were proud of his success and hinted that perhaps on his birthday he might receive a nice gift, maybe a book about

Roman history. But Edward knew they would never be able to afford such a nice one as the one his teacher had given to the other boy.

During this time, Edward's uncle was staying with the family for a few weeks while he recuperated from an operation. He was gentle and serious, and kind to Edward. Edward had quickly become very attached to Uncle Luke, and they spent a lot of time together.

At the moment Uncle Luke was seated under a fine old oak tree. The countryside made a lovely scene.

In the distance lay the ocean, its deep green waters contrasting with the pale blue sky filled with thin white clouds. Uncle Luke held a book in his hand, and seemed to be engrossed in his reading. Edward approached hesitantly, not wishing to disturb his uncle, yet wanting to speak with him. When Uncle Luke looked up and noticed his nephew, he smiled and beckoned him to come.

"How are you feeling?" asked Edward politely.

"Fine," answered Uncle Luke. "I love to sit here and enjoy the view."

"What are you reading?" questioned Edward.

"It is a Bible, God's Word. One of the things I love about the Bible is the descriptions of nature it contains."

"I like reading the Bible, too," said Edward, somewhat defensively. "I won a prize for memorizing a lot of Bible verses last year."

"I'm glad to hear that," smiled Uncle Luke. "But what gave you greater satisfaction, the Bible verses or the prize you won?"

Edward looked uncomfortable and did not reply.

"It is good to be happy with a prize, since you earned it," explained Uncle Luke. "I understand you won a prize today for your good grade on your history exam."

"Yes, but it wasn't the prize I wanted," complained Edward. "There was a book I really, really wanted, but I didn't get it. It was worth just as much as the Bible I got."

"What do you mean?"

"Well, John got the same grade I did, and Mr. Howard gave him the history book. It just would have been better to give that book to me since I would have appreciated it more than John does. John doesn't even care that much about history."

"Do you already have your own Bible?" asked Uncle Luke.

"No, but I just use the Bible in the living room."

Uncle Luke paged through his Bible and pointed to Deuteronomy 6:6. "Start reading here."

Edward read: "And these words, which I command thee this day, shall be in thine heart: and thou shalt teach them diligently unto thy children, and shalt talk of them when thou sittest in thine house, and when thou walkest by the way, and when thou liest down, and when thou risest up. And thou shalt bind them for a sign upon thine hand, and they shall be as frontlets between thine eyes. And thou shalt write them upon the posts of thy house, and on thy gates" (Deuteronomy 6:6-9).

"To whom was this command given, Edward?"

"To the Israelites."

"Yes," said Uncle Luke, "but the Word of God is as much binding on us as on them, in everything except the sacrifices and ceremonies."

"Are we commanded to write the Bible on our

hands and on our doorposts?" asked Edward in surprise.

"No, my dear boy," replied Uncle Luke, "not literally. What this passage in Deuteronomy says to us is that we must have the Word of God continually on our minds. And how do you suppose we get our thoughts to be so occupied with the Bible?"

"By reading it, I guess," answered Edward grudgingly.

"By reading it often, and meditating on it much," said Uncle Luke. "Without prayer and meditation and the working of the Holy Spirit, we cannot obtain any spiritual blessing, much less obey the commands of Scripture. And without reading the Bible you will have little desire to pray. We are like people wandering in the dark, while the Bible is as a bright lamp held out to direct us in the only safe path. You cannot be a child of God if you do not do His will. You cannot do His will unless you know it, and it is by the Bible that God is pleased to communicate that knowledge. Do you begin to see, Edward, that the Bible is more valuable than that wonderful history book?"

"Yes, I do," admitted Edward, "but the Bible is such a solemn book, and if I read it all the time, I will never be happy."

"There is no happiness among the lost, Edward," replied Uncle Luke. "It would be dreadful if you were to neglect your soul and the salvation that is to be found in God's Word. Besides, it is not true at all that those who read the Bible are unhappy. It is exactly the opposite: those who love God's Word are very happy! I know people who were sad before they started to read the Bible, and have become cheerful and happy by studying it. Never in my life have I known a person who was sorry that he started studying the Bible."

Edward thought for a moment, and then said, "I remember one of the Bible verses I learned. 'Her ways are ways of pleasantness, and all her paths are peace. She is a tree of life to them that lay hold upon her: and happy is every one that retaineth her' (Proverbs 3:17-18). I think the woman represents wisdom."

"That's right, Wisdom is the Lord Jesus Christ," explained Uncle Luke. "'And the work of righteousness shall be peace; and the effect of righteousness quietness and assurance for ever. And my people shall dwell in a peaceable habitation, and in sure dwellings, and in quiet resting places' (Isaiah 32:17-18). 'And the ransomed of the LORD shall return, and come to Zion with songs and everlasting joy upon their heads: they shall obtain joy and gladness, and sorrow and sighing shall flee away' (Isaiah 35:10). Does this sound gloomy to you?"

"Not at all. I often wondered why you would want to read the Bible when you were feeling sick, Uncle Luke. I thought it would be better to read something else, because I thought the Bible would make you feel sad."

"How can I feel sad when the Bible tells me that all these things are working together for my spiritual good (Romans 8:28)? The Bible tells me that God, 'who spared not his own Son, but delivered him up for us all, how shall he not with him also freely give us all things?' (Romans 8:32). When I think of what I deserve because of my sins, and see the Lamb of God bearing the chastisement that should fall on me, how can I be sad? When I feel that the Holy Spirit is bringing these things to my remembrance, and enabling me to love the Lord Jesus who has done so much for me, shouldn't I rejoice? I do grieve, though, Edward, because of my many offenses against God, but I am assured that Christ's blood cleanses me from all sin, and that in Him I have a powerful Advocate with the Father. After I die, my body will return to dust, but I will enter into the presence of my Redeemer and rejoice there forever."

Edward looked at his uncle. His eyes were shining with tears, but they were tears of joy. His happiness was obvious, and for the first time in his life, Edward felt a twinge of jealousy toward God's children.

"Uncle Luke," he said. "It is wrong of me not to want to read the Bible. I see now why it is more valuable than that history book. I didn't like it when the Bible talks about sin and its consequences. But I see now how important it is to read it every day. Could we read it together every day, Uncle Luke?"

"I would be delighted," smiled the man happily. "And we will pray together that the Holy Spirit blesses our reading."

So, every day, when Edward came home from school, he ran to find his uncle sitting under the beautiful oak tree, and together they read from the gift Bible that Edward had earned. Through God's grace and the working of the blessed Spirit, Edward received a gift he had not earned—the salvation of his soul. He learned about the sinfulness of his own nature and his utter inability to save himself (and this made him sad), but he also learned the joy that the forgiveness of sin gives (and this made him very, very happy).

—12—
Trying to Enter by the Wrong Door

*Humble yourselves in the sight of the Lord,
and he shall lift you up.*
—James 4:10

Robert Murray M'Cheyne of Dundee was a well-known preacher in Scotland. He was known for his holy life and powerful preaching. Once, during one of his sermons, a man who had been anxious about his soul for a long time was blessed with peace from the Holy Spirit. At the close of the service, the man went to Rev. M'Cheyne to tell him the good news. It was clear on the man's face that the Lord had given him peace. The joy of the Lord so filled the man's soul that Rev. M'Cheyne did not even ask if the Lord had forgiven his sins. He simply asked, "How did you get it?"

The man answered, "All the time I have been trying to enter by the *saint's* door, but while you were preaching, I saw my mistake and entered in at the *sinner's* door."

Many people make the same mistake. They try to make themselves better for God, at the same time turning their back on the door to Christ. Jesus said, "They that are whole need not a physician; but they that are sick. I came not to call the righteous, but sinners to repentance" (Luke 5:31-32). "The Son of man is come to seek and to save that which was lost" (Luke 19:10).

Children, do not try to make yourself "presentable" or "acceptable" to God. You will never succeed. Come to Him as a sinner, not as a saint. Come as you are; come by faith. Come, trusting in Jesus Christ, and you will receive a free, full, and eternal salvation.

—13—
Jack and His Master

*For we which live are alway delivered unto death for Jesus'
sake, that the life also of Jesus might be made manifest in
our mortal flesh.*
—2 Corinthians 4:11

 When Jack was a boy, there were no
religious people in his area. He had,
however, a young master about his age,
who went to school. Master Evan liked
Jack, and, realizing Jack was interested
in books, he promised to teach him what he knew.
Every evening, Master Evan would come down to the
kitchen, where he would teach Jack what he had
learned that day. This is how it came about that a
slave on the Gray Plantation learned to read.

When the boys were about fifteen years old, they
began reading out of a New Testament that Master
Evan had earned. They decided to take turns reading, verse by verse, each correcting the other when
one of them made a mistake.

Not only did the boys learn to read well, but the
Holy Spirit taught them the truth of what they were
reading. They both began to feel that they were sinners
before God, and they saw the need for seeking the sal-

vation of their souls. Two teenagers, seeking forgiveness of their sins, searching the Scriptures, with no one to guide them but the Holy Spirit, found grace in the eyes of the Lord. He heard their prayers, and forgave them their sins. They were taught that they were righteous only in the blood of the Lord Jesus.

The result of this was that Jack began to hold meetings for prayer and Bible reading among the slaves. He wanted to share this wonderful news of salvation with his family and fellow workers. When Evan's father, Master Gray, found out about the meetings, he was very angry. He was especially angry because his son had been converted and was now "religious." He forbade Jack to hold any more meetings or to speak with his son, saying that if he did, he would be severely beaten for it.

Jack, however, believed it was more important to tell the slaves about the Lord Jesus Christ than to spare his body. He continued to hold meetings on Sundays. On Monday mornings Master Gray would tie him up and whip him. His back was badly cut with the cowhide whip the master used. Every Sabbath Jack would preach, and every Monday he would be beaten. His back never had time to heal between the whippings, and he had to do his daily work in a great deal of pain.

Life went on this way for about a year and a half. One Monday morning, Master Gray, as usual, had made Jack's fellow slaves tie him to a tree in the yard

after stripping the shirt off his back. It was a beautiful morning in the summer time, and the sun shone
brightly. Everything around seemed very pleasant.

Master Gray came up to Jack with slow strides,
took his stand, and looked at him closely. He made
no move to lift the whip in his hand. His conscience
was at work. "Well, Jack," he said, "your back is covered all over with scars and sores, and I see no place
to begin to whip you. You stubborn wretch, how long
do you intend to go on in this way?"

"Just as long as the Lord will let me live, master,"
was Jack's meek reply.

"But what is your purpose in all this nonsense?"

Jack turned slightly to look at his master. "In the
morning of the resurrection, when my poor body
shall rise from the grave, I intend to
show these scars to my heavenly
Father. They are witnesses of my
faithfulness to His cause."

There was silence as Jack
turned his face again to the tree,
waiting for the blows of the
whip. The stillness was broken
when Master Gray ordered the
attending slaves to untie Jack.
"Go and hoe the weeds in the
corn field," he said sharply,
then turned and walked
toward the big house.

Late in the evening, as the shadows were beginning to stretch over the field, Master Gray came toward the corn field, pulling a weed here and a weed there, until he reached Jack.

"Come here, Jack," ordered Master Gray. "Sit down."

Jack obediently sat where his master pointed. Master Gray sat next to him on a tree stump. He sighed. "Jack, I want you to tell me the truth. For a long time your back has been sore from my whip. You have had to work very hard, and you are only a poor slave. Tell me, are you happy or not?"

Jack's eyes brightened. "Yes, master, I believe I am as happy as I can be on this earth."

"Well, Jack," confessed the old master, "I am not happy." He stared out over the corn fields. Nervously, he wiped his forehead. "Religion, you say, teaches you to pray for those who have hurt you." His voice grew soft and he stammered, "Would you—could you—I mean—would you be willing to pray for your old master, Jack?"

"Yes, with all my heart," answered the slave without a trace of bitterness.

They knelt down together in the dirt, and Jack prayed for Master Gray. Day after day, the master came to see the slave. Day after day, they prayed together in the field, until Master Gray found forgiveness and peace in the blood of the precious Lamb of God.

During these days and weeks, a special bond grew

between Jack and Master Gray. The rich plantation owner faithfully attended the slave church, gladly hearing Jack bring the Word of God every Sunday.

Jack had not been allowed to associate with his boyhood friend, Master Evan. But now, the friendship was encouraged. The Lord blessed Jack's ministry to rich and poor alike.

Years later, Old Master Gray lay on his deathbed. In one of his visits to his master's bedside, Jack received a gift: the gift of freedom. "Go on preaching as long as you live, Jack," said the dying man. "You have served me well. Now I give you your freedom so that you can bring the Word of God to people every day of the week. And I think, not too long from now, we will meet again in heaven."

—14—
A New Year's Start for Eternity

When thou vowest a vow unto God, defer not to pay it; for he hath no pleasure in fools: pay that which thou hast vowed.

—Ecclesiastes 5:4

It is not a pleasant thing for an unconverted person to look at the picture of his soul as shown in the album of God's Word. The first time Gordon ever experienced the truth of God's Word was one day when, as a boy, he looked for a few minutes in his Bible. Something that he read in those few minutes, from Psalm 36:1-4,[1] convinced him instantly that God knew him far better than he knew himself. The thought that he could learn what he was from the Word of God was something new to him and made him very uncomfortable. Quickly shutting the Bible, he laid it aside, and for a long time afterward he could not bear to open it.

Once, as Gordon was going to school, a neighbor spoke to him about his soul's salvation. He was so impressed with the need to be saved, that he resolved to become a Christian. By the time he returned home after a busy day at school, however, all his good intentions had vanished.

This was not the first time Gordon had made a resolution to seek the Lord. His parents were godly people, and Gordon faithfully attended church and Sunday school. He knew that he needed a new heart. Sometimes he had impressions and would think more seriously about his soul. But soon his thoughts were filled again with fun and games.

Some years later, at the age of sixteen, Gordon left his home in Scotland to work as an apprentice on board a ship. He was eager to learn everything he could about ships and sailing. But as soon as he discovered that life aboard ship was hard and often monotonous, he changed his mind. The life of a

sailor was not what he wanted after all. He decided to run away from the ship.

So, one night, while the ship lay in the harbor of San Francisco, California, Gordon packed his suitcase and stealthily left. He soon found a place to stay, but he had to give the landlady all the money he had to pay for his room a week in advance. Satisfied, she showed him to a little room, then closed the door and left.

Instead of feeling relieved, however, Gordon felt afraid. He was far from home, in a big city, without friends, money, or food. Who would help him? How would he get home? In a panic, he dropped to his knees beside the bed and vowed to God that if He would help him find a job, he would serve Him for the rest of his life.

The next day, Gordon found a job, which brought him a good wage. After a few months of saving, he had enough to get home to his family in Scotland. But did he remember his vow? Sadly, no. Gordon forgot the God who had been so good to him.

After a year at home, Gordon became restless. While working in San Francisco, he had made some friends and he decided to visit them. It was the year 1890, and long trips were not easily made. But Gordon was young, and by springtime he had enough money for another trip across the ocean. His friends welcomed him enthusiastically. They invited him to join them at their parties and other evenings of "fun."

The months flew by, and the year was coming to a close. Michael, one of his friends, invited Gordon and the others to an elaborate New Year's Eve party at his luxurious home. Smiling, Gordon promised he would be there. This would be a party to remember!

He went home to dress up for the party. Since it was still early, he rested a while in a chair by the window of his hotel room. His thoughts drifted to his past life. He was not happy. The thrill of spending time with his friends was not as great as he had hoped it would be. He felt sad and empty. The parties, the fun, and his many travels did not satisfy him. He no longer attended church, and he cringed to think what his parents would say if they knew about his lifestyle. The sinfulness of his life came up before him, and he realized that he was wandering farther and farther away from God. The thought flashed into his mind, "Where will it all end?"

Gordon had to admit that he knew the answer to that dreadful question, and it filled him with misery. He decided he would turn over a new leaf. He was just beginning to feel pleased with himself at this resolution when he remembered other times in his life when he had made similar resolutions. He had turned over many "new leaves" before, and the new leaves were soon as black as the old ones. What good would a new resolution do?

His thoughts turned to his mother in Scotland. She had written often to him and pleaded with him to flee from sin to the Savior. She generally wrote these warnings at the end of her letters, and, as much as he loved his mother's letters, he could not bear to read those warnings, so lovingly given. He thought about the God his parents served. What must God think of him? Would He be willing to help him now after his life of sin and his many broken promises?

Ashamed, and not knowing what to say, Gordon could only weep as he prayed, "Oh God, help me!" For five hours he sat in the chair by the window, his thoughts and prayers mixed together. Sometimes he felt hopeless, knowing he did not deserve God's mercy. At other times, he pleaded for God to forgive

his sins, filled with sorrow at the thought of his wicked life. The reality of eternity overwhelmed him. He was not prepared to meet God!

At last he glanced at his watch. He had completely forgotten about the New Year's Eve party at Michael's house. It was near midnight. Suddenly, he remembered that his church in Scotland held services as the old year faded into the new one. He wondered if any churches in San Francisco followed the same practice. Pulling on his coat, he decided to find out.

After a short walk, he found an open church. Taking a seat in the back, Gordon listened intently. A young man was preaching. In a plain, straightforward sermon, he told his audience that Christ came to save helpless sinners. His text was Hebrews 9:14: "How much more shall the blood of Christ, who through the eternal Spirit offered himself without spot to God, purge your conscience from dead works to serve the living God?" Immediately, it occurred to Gordon that Jesus could save him, too! With an overflowing heart, Gordon, by grace, trusted in the only Savior of sinners, the Lord Jesus Christ. He went home with a sweet, humble joy in his heart. As he walked back to his room in the hotel, he heard people celebrating the new year, but Gordon's joy was deeper, and though it was often dimmed by sin and sorrow, this joy remained with him till he died. By grace, he learned the truth of some of the other verses in Psalm 36: "How excellent is thy loving kindness, O God! therefore the children of men put their trust under the shadow of thy wings. They shall be abundantly satisfied with the fatness of thy house; and thou shalt make them drink of the river of thy pleasures. For with thee is the fountain of life: in thy light shall we see light" (Psalm 36:7-9).

Gordon learned that no resolution he made, no matter how sincere, could ever save him. Only the blood of the Lord Jesus Christ saves from sin. He alone can save, sanctify, and satisfy. Have you made resolutions like Gordon? "No conviction, however deep, however grand, however solemn, can save," wrote Gordon to his parents. "Christ alone, Christ alone, Christ alone can save."

---

[1] "The transgression of the wicked saith within my heart, that there is no fear of God before his eyes. For he flattereth himself in his own eyes, until his iniquity be found to be hateful. The words of his mouth are iniquity and deceit: he hath left off to be wise, and to do good. He deviseth mischief upon his bed; he setteth himself in a way that is not good; he abhorreth not evil."

—15—
Clean Within

Purge me with hyssop, and I shall be clean: wash me, and I shall be whiter than snow.... Create in me a clean heart, O God; and renew a right spirit within me.

—Psalm 51:7, 10

"Mommy," said Katie to her mother one day, "would you tell me how I can be good inside?"

"What do you mean?" asked her mother, surprised by the unusual question.

"I mean that I don't have right feelings in my heart. Daddy tells me I am a good girl, and you call me 'sweetheart.' Everybody thinks I'm good, but I'm not good at all!"

"I'm sorry to hear it," answered Katie's mother.

"So am I," said Katie. "I know my heart is very wicked." Tears filled Katie's eyes. "Yesterday, when I was wearing my favorite dress, I wanted to go for a ride with you and Daddy. He told me that he wanted to spend time with you and that I could go some other time. I went back into the house and waited for you to come back. Aunt Lydia told you I had been very good about it. But she didn't know! I didn't say anything to her, but I went upstairs, and even though I didn't cry, I thought very mean things. I punched my pillow because I was so angry, and I wished the car would break down so you couldn't go for a ride!"

Katie was crying now, and she added in a sob, "Mommy, can't you tell me how I can be good inside?"

Katie's mother hugged her daughter as she explained that Jesus shed His blood to wash away sin. She told Katie that our hearts are like fountains which continually flow with sin. If we want to be clean inside, we need to have the fountain of sin stopped, and that can only happen by God's almighty power. We need a new heart, a heart that is cleansed from sin. God promises to give this: "A new heart also will I give you, and a new spirit will I put within you: and I will take away the stony heart out of your flesh, and I will give you an heart of flesh. And I will put my Spirit within you, and cause you to walk in my statutes, and ye shall keep my judgments, and do them" (Ezekiel 36:26-27). When Jesus determines to save His people, He always begins with the heart. When our hearts are cleansed, then we will obey the Lord and walk in His ways. If you can make a fountain pure, then you may be sure that the streams which flow out from it will be pure also. But we must ask for this gift. God says,

"Thus saith the Lord GOD; I will yet for this be inquired of by the house of Israel, to do it for them" (Ezekiel 36:37). The Lord wants to give you a new heart, but He also wants you to ask Him for it. And He promises that "those that seek me early shall find me" (Proverbs 8:17).

The Holy Spirit was teaching Katie that even though she could keep her lips from saying bad things, she couldn't stop her heart from thinking and feeling bad things. She could be good on the outside, but she was wicked on the inside. After this talk with her mother, the Holy Spirit taught Katie to believe in Jesus Christ, who takes away sin, and makes hearts clean within.

—16—
The Bird in the Church

I am the door: by me if any man enter in, he shall be saved, and shall go in and out, and find pasture.

—John 10:9

In the center of a large early American town stood a beautiful church. Though America was still a young country, the church was about two hundred years old, one of the first churches built in the New Land. It was surrounded by many trees. High above the tallest buildings rose a tall steeple in which a large clock solemnly chimed the hours. What was even better than its outward beauty, this church had been a true house of worship, where God was worshiped in Spirit and in truth.

One beautiful Sunday morning in late spring, the doors of the church had been left open during the service to allow the fresh breezes in, though the windows remained closed. Just before the service, a bird swooped through the open door and flew up to the vaulted roof. Alarmed by the sight of so many people, and the voices and the music which it heard, it desperately tried to escape.

In one of the pews sat a young lady, who noticed

the frightened bird. Her gaze followed the fluttering creature from window to window as it vainly sought to escape. It looked for an exit at every window. Then it rose to the ceiling, frantically trying to find a way out of the building. At last, its wings grew weary, and all hope of escape seemed gone. As if unable to keep itself in flight much longer, the little bird flew lower, just above the heads of the congregation. Just then it caught sight of the door, and, in a moment, it was free. The young lady couldn't help smiling as she heard the bird sing a happy song of triumph in the nearby branches of the trees.

When the bird had gone, the thoughts of the young woman turned to herself. Suddenly, she realized she was just like that little bird. "I have been acting like that foolish bird," she thought to herself. "I have been seeking peace in ways and places where there is no peace! I am trying to escape from the punishment of sin by beating against closed windows. I will never be able to pay for my own sin! Christ is the door! Through Him there is escape from sin and from the power of sin. I have acted like that foolish bird far too long. Just as it has escaped through the door of the church, I want to find peace through the Lord Jesus Christ."

From this day on, the Holy Spirit worked in this young lady's heart. She learned that she could never satisfy God by trying to pay for her sin. Her good works were stained with sin. She needed forgiveness and grace from the Lord Jesus Christ. By asking Him for mercy, she was knocking at the Door, and when He forgave her, she was set free.

What about you, children? Are you still beating at the windows, like this little bird, trying to find an escape from sin? Are you even trying to escape at all? Do you try to quiet your conscience by telling yourself that you have plenty of time to repent later, when you are older? Or, do you think you are not really so sinful, that God is kind, and He will overlook your flaws? Those are lies from Satan, and you must never believe them. You do not know how much time you will have; you are far more sinful than you think you are; and, though God is kind, He will not, and cannot overlook any sin! Flee to the Lord Jesus Christ, the open Door! Tell Him your sins. You may even tell Him that you don't think you are all that wicked, but then ask the Holy Spirit to show you your sins so that you may hurry through the Door and find true peace and freedom in the Lord Jesus Christ. "Then said Jesus unto them again, Verily, verily I say unto you, I am the door of the sheep" (John 10:7).

—17—
A Search for Atoning Blood

Forasmuch as ye know that ye were not redeemed with corruptible things, as silver and gold, from your vain conversation received by tradition from your fathers; but with the precious blood of Christ, as of a lamb without blemish and without spot.

—1 Peter 1:18, 19

In the spring of 1898, an evangelist was holding some gospel meetings in San Francisco. He had a special interest in the salvation of the Jews, and had just returned from a trip to Israel. Now he was giving presentations in various churches around the city. His purpose was to prove from Scripture that Jesus Christ is indeed the Messiah. Once, when he finished his speech, he asked if there were any questions, or if anyone had a testimony. He especially welcomed Jews to ask questions. At last an old man stood up and told his story.

"This is Passover week among you, my Jewish brethren," he said, "and as I sat here, I was thinking

how you will be observing it. You will put away all
leaven from your houses; you will eat the matzah
(unleavened wafers) and the roasted lamb. You will
attend synagogue services, and carry out the ritual
and directions of the Talmud.[1]

"But you forget, my brethren, that you have
everything except that which Jehovah required first
of all. He did not say, 'When I see the leaven put
away, or, when I see you eat the matzah, or the lamb,
or go to the synagogue, I will pass over you,' but His
Word says, 'When I see the *blood*, I will pass over
you, and the plague shall not be upon you to destroy
you, when I smite the land of Egypt' (Exodus 12:13,
emphasis mine). Ah, my brethren, you can substitute nothing for this. You must have the blood!"

After a moment's pause, the old man went on,
"I was born in Palestine, nearly 70 years ago. As a
child, I was taught to read the Law, the Psalms, and
the Prophets. I attended the synagogue, and learned
Hebrew from the Rabbis. At first I believed what I
was told, that ours was the true and only religion,
but as I grew older and studied the Law more
intently, I was struck by the place that blood had in
all the ceremonies, and was equally struck by its
utter absence in the rituals with which I was brought
up. Again and again I read Exodus 12, and Leviticus
16 and 17. The latter chapters made me tremble, as
I thought of the great Day of Atonement, and the
importance of the blood. Day and night one verse

would ring in my ears, 'It is the blood that maketh an atonement for the soul' (Leviticus 17:11b). I knew I had broken the Law. I needed atonement. Year after year, on that day, I beat my breast as I confessed my need of it, but it had to be made by blood, and there was no blood!

"In my distress, I at last opened my heart to a learned and respected Rabbi. He told me that God was angry with His people. Jerusalem was in the hands of the Gentiles, the temple was destroyed, and an Islamic mosque was built in its place. Jerusalem is the only place on earth where we dare shed the sacrifice, in accordance with Leviticus 17 and Deuteronomy 12, but it had been desecrated, and our nation scattered. That was why there was no blood, the Rabbi explained to me. God Himself had closed the way to carry out the solemn service of the great Day of Atonement. Now, we must turn to the Talmud, and rest on its instruction, and trust in the mercy of God and the merits of the fathers.

"I tried to be satisfied, but could not. Something seemed to tell me that the Law was unchanged, even though our temple was destroyed. Nothing else but blood could atone for the soul. We Jews dared not shed blood for atonement anywhere else but in the place the Lord had chosen: 'But in the place which the LORD shall choose in one of thy tribes, there thou shalt offer thy burnt offerings, and there thou shalt do all that I command thee' (Deuteronomy

12:14). So we were left without an atonement at all, I reasoned. This thought filled me with horror. I consulted other Rabbis with my burning question, 'Where can I find the blood of the atonement?' But no one had an answer.

"I was over thirty years old when I left Palestine and came to Constantinople[2] with my soul exceedingly troubled about my sins. One evening, I was walking down one of the narrow streets of that city, when I saw a sign informing passersby about a meeting for Jews. Curiosity led me to open the door and go in. Just as I took a seat, I heard a man say, 'The blood of Jesus Christ his Son cleanseth us from all sin' (1 John 1:7). It was my first introduction to the gospel. I listened breathlessly as the speaker told how God had declared that 'without shedding of blood is no remission' (Hebrews 9:12b) or forgiveness of sins, but that He had given His only begotten Son, the Lamb of God, to die. All who trust in His blood are forgiven all their iniquities. This was the Messiah of Isaiah 53; this was the Sufferer of Psalm 22! Suddenly it all made sense. My long search was over. I had found the blood of atonement at last! I trusted then and there in the blood of the Son of God! Finally I had peace in my heart because I knew my sins were forgiven."

The old man now appealed to the Jews in the audience. Tears streamed down his cheeks as he pleaded with them to believe in Jesus Christ, the Messiah. "His blood has been shed for sinners. It has satisfied God, or He would not have raised Christ from the dead, and it is the only means of salvation for either Jew or Gentile. Dear brethren, the Messiah has come! He has made atonement with His blood. Turn to Him and acknowledge Him as the 'Lamb of God who taketh away the sin of the world' (John 1:29b). You will have no peace or salvation until you trust in Him."

Children, have you found the blood of atonement? Are you trusting in God's smitten Lamb? Or, are you trusting in your good works, your church attendance, Bible reading and prayers, or your good behavior? All these things are necessary, but they do not provide the blood of atonement. Flee to Jesus Christ with all your sins, for only in Him is found forgiveness of sin.

---

[1] Talmud: Jewish sacred writings compiled between the Babylonian captivity and the close of the canon of Scripture, but neither the Old Testament nor the New.

[2] Constantinople is now Istanbul, Turkey.

—18—
"Can I Become a Christian?"

*For whosoever shall call upon the name
of the Lord shall be saved.*
—Romans 10:13

In the winter of 1852, a teacher named Mr. John Cooper worked in the school and Sunday School of a town in America. One of his students was a girl named Mary. From her earliest years, Mary's parents had treated her harshly and forced her to work hard. She received no thanks or affection from her family. There was no time to play or make friends. Because Mary's family did not attend church, she did not know the Lord, and she had no one to whom to tell her troubles.

Mary grew into a young lady. She was well behaved and polite, and seemed to have overcome her difficult past. No one knew, however, that in the darkness of the night, she would often cry herself to sleep. She was a very unhappy girl.

One day, Mary stayed after school to finish copying an assignment from the chalkboard. The teacher used this opportunity to speak with Mary about her need of salvation. Mr. Cooper told her that she was a sinner who needed to be washed in the blood of the Lord Jesus. Mary listened politely, but made no answer.

Mary was very good at covering up her feelings. She had learned at a very young age to hide her feelings to avoid punishment. Mr. Cooper only saw her expressionless face; he did not know the thoughts that tumbled through Mary's mind. He did not realize that she was angry. She hated Mr. Cooper. Why did he talk to her like that? Everyone thought she and her family were wicked people because they did not go to church. Religious people like Mr. Cooper thought they were better than Mary. Well, she didn't want to hear what he had to say. She tried to push Mr. Cooper's words out of her memory.

Soon after this, Mary and her family moved away, and Mr. Cooper did not see her for several years. Mary was glad to get away from her teacher. But God, in His providence, arranged that Mary would visit her hometown, and meet Mr. Cooper again. Making use of an opportunity to speak with Mary privately, Mr. Cooper once again spoke to her about her soul, urging her to repent and believe. His words were gentle, and his tone sincere as he told her about the loving Savior.

This time Mary's response was different. She

covered her face in her hands, and with tears in her eyes, lamented, "Can *I* become a Christian?"

She told Mr. Cooper that no one had ever spoken to her about her need for salvation, and she felt she was too wicked to find forgiveness with God. All these years, since Mr. Cooper had spoken to her, the Holy Spirit had been stirring Mary's conscience. She could never rid herself of his admonitions. Now God brought her face to face with her need. For

days, she was in great distress, not daring to reject the gospel, yet fearing the promises were not for her.

Meanwhile, Mr. Cooper and the other Sunday school teachers prayed earnestly for Mary's salvation, wrestling with heartfelt pleadings at the throne of grace. God heard and answered their prayers. Mary began to hope in the power of Jesus' blood, and trusted in Him for her salvation. More and more, she desired to devote herself to the service of the Lord.

Over the years, Mary observed the Christians with whom she came into contact. Although she tried to avoid them, she couldn't help wondering about these people. She gradually realized that their joy was real, not a flimsy, groundless emotion. She became jealous. But then she worried that these joys could never be for her. She hadn't wanted to listen to God. Was it too late?

As Mary struggled and her friends prayed, the Holy Spirit showed her "the Lamb of God, which taketh away the sin of the world" (John 1:29b). A new life was given to Mary, and she now understood the deep, thankful joy that all true believers experience.

Mary, who had been hopeless and angry, through the saving work of the Holy Spirit, became joyful and happy. Not long after this, she went back to school. Her greatest desire was to use her talents to honor the Lord. She became a teacher, just like her new friend, Mr. Cooper! She loved to tell her students about her favorite teacher, who had taught her the most valuable things of all. He had pointed her to the Lord Jesus Christ, who welcomes sinners, no matter how wicked.

Have you been born again? Do you know the joy of true thanksgiving for all that God has done for you, especially salvation? Are you one of God's children? "Thou wilt show me the path of life: in thy presence is fulness of joy; at thy right hand there are pleasures for evermore" (Psalm 16:11).

—19—
Little Johnny's First Bible

Thy word was unto me the joy and rejoicing of my heart;
for I am called by thy name, O LORD God of hosts.
—Jeremiah 15:16b

Johnny lived in Scotland. He did not care much for toy shops and candy stores, but he could never pass a bookshop without wishing he had money to buy something. His little library at home consisted of all kinds of storybooks, but lately, he had begun to long for a Bible of his own. His parents read aloud from the family Bible every day, and they spoke to their children about Jesus and their need to be cleansed by His blood. Johnny thought often of their loving words and asked the Lord to give him a new heart. A love for the Lord and for His Word was born in his young heart.

In those days in Scotland, everyone would go to church carrying a Bible. They would not think of going to church without their Bibles any more than going without their coats. All Johnny's brothers had Bibles to take to church and Sunday school, so why not he? Now that he was five years old, he felt himself old enough to have his own Bible. He must get a Bible—but how, he did not know. It would be no use, he knew, to ask his mother for one. She would say he was too young, and that his brothers were seven before they got theirs. Johnny decided that he would save up his money until he had enough to buy a Bible, and he determined not to go near a bookstore so he wouldn't be tempted to spend his money on other books.

So, Johnny saved his money. He asked his parents and neighbors if he could do little chores for them to earn a little money. Often he would empty his piggy bank and pour the money on his bed to carefully count. It seemed the day would never come when he would have enough to buy a Bible. The months passed, and Johnny kept saving. He bought no candy or toys or other books. Finally, on a bright Saturday morning, Johnny told his mother that he wanted to visit the bookshop and that he would be back soon. He did not tell her what he was going to buy; he wanted to surprise her. He skipped happily down the few blocks to the bookstore. He pulled open the heavy door and went inside. After his eyes adjusted to the dim light, he politely asked Mr. Knight, "Sir, do you have any Bibles today?"

"A Bible!" exclaimed Mr. Knight. "Can you read the Bible already?"

"I know some of the words, but not all of them," Johnny admitted.

"What kind of Bible do you wish to buy?"

"A pocket Bible, sir, so I can take it to church with me."

The shopkeeper showed Johnny a very plain black Bible. "How about this one?" he asked.

"No, thank you," answered Johnny. "I'd like a really nice one."

He showed Johnny several little Bibles, and Johnny chose the most expensive one. Mr. Knight gave the little boy a searching look, and said, "Are you able to pay for such an expensive Bible?"

"Yes, sir!" responded Johnny confidently.

"Where did you get the money? Did your mother give it to you?"

"No, sir," answered Johnny. "I...."

"Does she know that you are buying an expensive Bible?"

The little boy's eyes filled with tears. This was not what he expected! "No."

"Did you get the money honestly? Or did you steal it?"

This was too much for Johnny's honest heart. He burst into tears, all the time trying to speak, but he could not. Mr. Knight put Johnny's money on the counter. "I see how it is. Go home and tell your mother to come and see me," he said sternly.

Johnny realized that Mr. Knight thought he had stolen the money! He ran home, threw himself into his mother's arms, crying and unable to speak. His mother was alarmed, and begged him to tell her what had happened. She began to unbutton his shirt to find out where he was hurt. He took her hands in his little ones, and shook his head. "No, Mommy!" he finally managed to say between sobs.

His mother had become almost frantic, so great were Johnny's tears. "What is it, then? My dear little one, try to tell me what's wrong!"

At last she made out a few words, "Knight— Bible—money—thief."

"You went to Mr. Knight's bookstore, and you wanted to buy a Bible?"

Johnny nodded, still sobbing.

"Did he think you had stolen the money?"

Johnny only cried harder.

Her own eyes filling with sympathetic tears, she took her youngest child on her lap and gently rocked him, stroking his head and back, comforting him until he grew calm. Then he told her the whole story, how hard he had saved his money and how badly he wanted to buy a Bible because it is God's Word. Kissing him tenderly, she put him down on the sofa, and told Johnny she would be back in a little while. With firm steps, she made her way to the bookshop.

Mr. Knight saw that she had been crying, and stammered, "H-hello, ma'am. What can I do for you?"

"I'm Johnny's mother. He was here a little while ago to purchase a Bible."

The shopkeeper nervously explained what he had done, and why he did it. "I didn't think such a little boy would be able to save up so much money on his own. I've never seen anything like it."

"Yes," smiled the woman. "I haven't either. But, you see, Mr. Knight, Johnny loves the Lord. That's why he wants a Bible so badly. He has worked odd jobs around the neighborhood and done without candy and new toys for a year now so that he could buy a copy of God's Word for himself. I am amazed at his determination. You broke his little heart when you accused him of stealing the money," she scolded gently.

"Johnny is not like my other boys," she continued. "He's always loved books. He could read by the age of four. To be able to read the Bible whenever and wherever he wants is his dearest wish."

As she spoke, Mr. Knight's eyes also filled with tears, and he apologized many times. "I had no idea, ma'am," he said, "I'm so sorry. Poor little boy."

"You couldn't have known," answered Johnny's mother kindly.

"You tell Johnny I'm sorry, ma'am," said Mr. Knight. "And could you send your little boy over here? I'd like to talk to him."

Johnny's anxious expression melted into a happy smile when his mother told him what had happened in the bookshop. "May I go right now, Mommy?"

"Of course," she smiled, giving him a hug.

As soon as Mr. Knight saw him, he took Johnny by the hand, patted his head, and asked his forgiveness. There were several customers in the store, and the shopkeeper introduced Johnny to them just like he was the most important client he had, and then told them Johnny's story. They all praised him, and complimented him on his wise choice, while Mr. Knight took down the Bible and wrapped it carefully. Coming around the counter, he handed Johnny the package, then reached into his pocket and returned the money to a very surprised little boy. "This is for you, my dear boy. Go home now to your mother. Keep the Bible for yourself, and read in it every day, and God will bless you. Keep the money, too; I will not take it from you after what I put you through. Come again soon, Johnny! I will not forget you."

Mr. Knight did not forget Johnny; the two became good friends, and Johnny went often to visit Mr. Knight at the bookshop even when he did not need to buy any books. God did indeed bless the reading of His Word to Johnny's heart. From a young age, he served the Lord. When he became a young man, he went to seminary and became a missionary so he could tell people in other countries about the Lord Jesus Christ.

Dear children, how do you spend your money? What do you wish for? Do you have a Bible, and do you read it? Take time to read your Bible, asking the Lord for His blessing, for by this Book you may be made wise unto salvation, through faith in Jesus Christ, and ready and able for every good word and work.

—20—
More About Johnny

Let no man despise thy youth; but be thou an example of
the believers, in word, in conversation, in charity, in spirit,
in faith, in purity.
—1 Timothy 4:12

Little Johnny's father died when Johnny was only
five years old. Sad to say, when he died, the
family stopped doing their family devotions. His older
brothers seemed content to continue life without
the prayers of their father, and although his mother
faithfully attended church, she did not seem to
understand the importance of family worship.
Johnny remembered how he had sat on his father's
knee at family worship as the praises of God were
sung, and how he had knelt by his chair as the family sent up their morning and evening prayers. The
more he read in the Bible, the more he longed to
have family worship once again, but he felt shy and
afraid to speak to his older brothers about it.

One day, Johnny found his mother alone in the
kitchen. Dusting off the family Bible, he opened it
to the book of Jeremiah. Thrusting the Book into
his mother's hands, he pointed with his finger to
this verse: "Pour out thy fury, O Lord, upon the hea-

then that know thee not, and upon the families that call not on thy name" (Jeremiah 10:25a). Johnny was too timid to read the verse aloud. After silently reading the verse, Johnny's mother looked at him sadly, her eyes filling with tears. She understood what he was trying to tell her, and felt the rebuke. Stroking his hair, she told him she would speak to his brothers when they came in, since it was their duty to lead family worship.

Johnny's mother did speak to his brothers, but they all refused. Instead of giving in to his brothers, however, Johnny reached a brave decision. After the evening meal, he took the Bible and the *Psalter*, and, looking to God for help, began to read aloud. Johnny's brothers rudely got up and left the room, leaving him and his mother to finish the devotions alone. In the morning they did the same, and con-

tinued to do so for a long time. They also began to
insult him, and mock him for his piety. Johnny was
shocked when his mother did not silence the boys,
even smiling at some of their jokes about her
youngest son. In spite of the mockery, Johnny
doggedly continued reading the Bible aloud, singing
a psalter, and then kneeling in prayer. Later, when
he was alone in his room, Johnny brought his pain
to his Savior, who understands what suffering is.
The little boy was comforted in knowing that he suf-
fered for his precious Lord, and was strengthened by
God's Word. "Take, my brethren, the prophets, who
have spoken in the name of the Lord, for an example of suffering affliction, and of patience. Behold,
we count them happy which endure. Ye have heard
of the patience of Job, and have seen the end of the
Lord; that the Lord is very pitiful, and of tender
mercy" (James 5:10, 11).

Throughout the two years this continued, the
Lord comforted and encouraged Johnny. "When
the poor and needy seek water, and there is none,
and their tongue faileth for thirst, I the LORD will
hear them, I the God of Israel will not forsake
them" (Isaiah 41:17). When some of Johnny's godly
friends and relatives learned of his solitary devotions, they offered that he could live with them.
After all, such a young boy should be sheltered and
nurtured in the faith, they reasoned. How could he
continue strong in the Lord with so much opposi-

tion? Many people might have given up hope, and stopped the attempts at family worship. Johnny's brothers continued their rudeness, and his mother often wished aloud that he would stop. But Johnny did not give up. He continued to pray and hope.

One morning, James, one of Johnny's brothers, remained seated as Johnny began to read, although he neither joined in the song of praise, nor knelt in prayer. Seeing James listen to Johnny as he read aloud, the other boys' consciences whispered that they should follow James' example. Though they tried to ignore their consciences, their jokes and insults faded, and eventually, the other brothers began to stay also, hiding behind the excuse that they wanted to keep James company. They took no part in the devotions, but merely sat quietly and listened. At last, one joined his voice in the song of praise, then another, and another. Soon after this, one knelt in prayer, shortly after that, another, then another, and then all the family were kneeling before God.

Not long afterwards, Johnny heard one of his brothers praying to God in his bedroom. The fear of God had entered the heart of this young man. This had a powerful effect on the rest of the family, and, one by one, the Holy Spirit touched each one of their hearts. Johnny's patient service to God was rewarded, and he had the happiness of seeing them all enter the kingdom of God, having given themselves, by the gracious work of the Spirit, to Christ and His church. Then each of the brothers took his turn in conducting family worship, and tried, by every act of kindness they could think of, to make up for their cruelty before. "For I will pour water upon him that is thirsty, and floods upon the dry ground: I will pour my spirit upon thy seed, and my blessing upon thine offspring.... One shall say, I am the LORD's; and another shall call himself by the name of Jacob; and another shall subscribe with his hand unto the LORD, and surname himself by the name of Israel" (Isaiah 44:3, 5).

When Johnny became a young man, God called him to become a missionary. As he was giving his mother a farewell hug, she said to him, "You are not my son only, but my spiritual father. I owe the salvation of my soul to you. I thank God that He has been pleased to use you for my salvation."

James told him, "If you had treated me the way I treated you for such a long time, I would still be on my way to destruction. It was your meekness and patience that first smote my heart and convicted my conscience."

The others agreed, "You are not only our natural brother, but our spiritual brother. We were saved not so much by what you said, as by your example."

For forty years Johnny preached the gospel faithfully and successfully in Scotland, Russia, England,

and America, supported and encouraged by the prayers of his beloved family.

The success which crowned Johnny's patience should encourage you to imitate his example, and to persist in prayer for yourselves, your parents, your brothers and sisters, and your friends. Children, you are neither too young nor too small to gain the attention of the heavenly Father. He hears your prayers, and loves to answer them, especially those which plead for the salvation of souls. Johnny gained a great reward for all his meekness and love which he showed to those who persecuted him. Ask the Lord for faith and endurance, because in your own strength, you will lose the battle. Johnny often fled to God in prayer, and spent many hours reading and studying his precious Bible. You must do the same. Will you "go and do...likewise" (Luke 10:37b)? Who will first dare to say, "I am the LORD's" (Isaiah 44:5a)? Many feel it is important to make a stand for the Lord, but they are waiting for others first to set the example, so that they may follow it. Paul said to the Thessalonians, "Not because we have not power, but to make ourselves an ensample unto you to follow us" (2 Thessalonians 3:9).

Salvation for your own soul is necessary before you can be an example for others. Do you love the Lord? Is it your desire to serve Him and speak well of Him to others? Wait no longer. Flee for your life. Through the irresistible work of the Spirit, those for whom you wait will follow right on after you, fleeing also from the wrath to come. The Lord promises to bless you in your service to Him. "Whosoever therefore shall confess me before men, him will I confess also before my Father which is in heaven" (Matthew 10:32). "Be strong and of a good courage, fear not, nor be afraid of them: for the LORD thy God, he it is that doth go with thee; he will not fail thee, nor forsake thee" (Deuteronomy 31:6).

—21—
True Safety

Thy words were found, and I did eat them; and thy word was unto me the joy and rejoicing of mine heart.

—Jeremiah 15:16a

Before the Reformation in 1517, most people belonged to the Roman Catholic Church. One of the beliefs of the priests was that ordinary people should not have Bibles. They told the people that the Bible was a very difficult book to understand, and that only very wise people like themselves were able to understand and explain the Word of God.

Of course, we know that this is not true. Certainly, some parts of the Bible are harder to understand than others, but the Holy Spirit is willing to teach anyone who comes to Him in faith. We believe what the Bible itself says, "Out of the mouth of babes and sucklings hast thou ordained strength" (Psalm 8:2a). The Lord Jesus Himself called little children to Himself, welcoming them. "Suffer the little children to come unto me, and forbid them not: for of such is the kingdom of God" (Mark 10:14b). This is an encouragement for you, children, to seek the Lord while you are young!

During this time, when Bibles were so rare, God

chose, in His sovereign good pleasure, to give a man and his wife a Bible. One day this man came home from work, and said to his wife, "I have something. You must tell no one, or we will be thrown into prison."

His wife was alarmed and asked what he had brought home. When the man took the Bible from under his shirt, the woman looked frightened. "You must get rid of it as quickly as you can! We may not own a Bible! It is not allowed!"

The man put the Bible behind the dresser. But he could not stop thinking about it. He began to read it. After several evenings of reading the Bible aloud, the man exclaimed, "Wife, if this book is true, we are *wrong!*"

He went on reading the Bible. He had no idea that all these things were in this forbidden Book! It showed him what a great sinner he was, and he became frightened. "Wife," he exclaimed, "if this book is true, we are *lost!*"

Still he continued to read the Bible. He began to love this Book. He learned to know and love the Lord Jesus. He found out that what the priests taught was not the way of salvation. Jesus Christ is the only Way of Life! "Wife," he cried, "if this book is true, we are *safe!*"

Together they rejoiced in the mercy and salvation that only God can give. That was a blessed discovery to make! Those who put their trust in Jesus will never be disappointed.

—22—
A Sermon in the Woods

The wind bloweth where it listeth, and thou hearest the sound thereof, but canst not tell whence it cometh, and whither it goeth: so is every one that is born of the Spirit.

—John 3:8

In a certain part of America, in a little town surrounded by woods, a minister of Jesus Christ was preaching the gospel to a group of villagers. It was in the early days of American history, when towns consisted of only a few log cabins, with fields painstakingly cut away from the surrounding forest. It was a rare privilege to have a visitor, much more so a preacher! The villagers gladly put aside their work and gathered to hear him.

Unnoticed by the group, a stranger on horseback, passing through the forest, heard the sound of the minister's voice. He stopped his horse, and then quietly urged his horse forward. Not wanting to be seen, the stranger kept himself hidden in the shadows of the trees, but ventured close enough to hear what the preacher was saying.

When the minister finished his sermon, the stranger just as quietly turned his horse around, and continued his journey without being noticed by the preacher and his audience. At the time, the message didn't seem all that special to the stranger, but he couldn't help thinking about what the minister had said. He had to admit that what he had just heard was true. As he rode along, and pondered the message of the gospel, the Spirit of God began to work in his heart. Like waves of the ocean, his sins seemed to wash over him, till he thought he would die of shame and guilt. He got off his horse and fell to the ground, pleading and crying for mercy. He felt he could not continue to live without God's mercy. Like Jacob, he cried, "I will not let thee go, except thou bless me" (Genesis 32:26b). How long he lay there, he did not know, but when he got up, he knew the Lord had answered his cries. He knew a wonderful change had taken place in his heart. No

longer overwhelmed with sin and guilt, his soul was flooded with love, peace, and sweet communion with God. He was a new creature in Christ Jesus.

He found his horse who had wandered off looking for grasses and water, and continued his journey, rejoicing in the goodness of God. Toward evening, he arrived at the next town. It was well-known for its wickedness, but the traveler needed a place to spend the night. He did not join the townspeople in their drinking and sinful talk, but boldly told them what great things the Lord had done for his soul. The people were astonished; they had never heard such things before. They didn't know what to make of it, and wondered aloud whether he was insane. They talked about locking him in the town jail. Hearing what they said, the traveler explained, with a beaming face, "Actually, I haven't been in my right mind until a few hours ago. Now I am set free, and I am very happy. Don't worry about me; I'm not insane!"

The stranger tried his best to relate to them what the traveling preacher had said in his sermon. He told them to flee from the wrath to come. The Spirit of God accompanied his earnest words, and many took the stranger's words to heart. They asked the traveler to stay awhile and tell them more of the things of God. His stay was greatly blessed: a revival began that day in the formerly wicked town, and many lost sinners were brought to salvation in Jesus Christ.

—23—
Debra's Plan

For the wages of sin is death; but the gift of God is eternal life through Jesus Christ our Lord.

—Romans 6:23

A little girl named Debra loved to play in the attic of her home. Debra's father stored extra lumber there so it would stay dry, and her mother stored canned fruits and vegetables for the winter. The rafters were hung with herbs and flowers to dry for later use. In the summer, the winter clothes and blankets were kept there. It was a wonderful place to play. One day, Debra noticed that her mother had canned some spiced apples—her favorite! There were several jars. Would Mommy notice if Debra opened just one jar? Her conscience told her that whether or not Mommy noticed, God certainly would, and that made her feel uncomfortable. Every time she went into the attic, however, those jars of spiced apples made her mouth water. Finally, she decided to open a can, just for one slice of apple. With a nail, she popped open the lid—did anyone hear it? With her fingers, she pulled out one of the beautiful pink rings and put it in her mouth. But somehow, it didn't taste nearly as good as it did last Christmas.

In the attic, hanging above the chests filled with blankets, was an old oil painting. The artist had skillfully painted a man's face, and it seemed that the eyes followed Debra's every move. She used to like the old man's picture, but now she wanted to get away from it. They seemed to scold her, "Oh, I see you, Debra! I saw what you did, and God saw it, too! He says, 'Be sure your sin will find you out'" (Numbers 32:23).

After several days, Debra became so annoyed, that she decided to put an end to the "sermon" these two great, staring eyes preached to her. She brought

into the attic a small pair of sharp, pointed scissors, climbed onto the trunks filled with blankets, and cut out the eyes in the painting. "There, now the old man can't scold me anymore!" she thought. But when she looked back at the painting, she saw two dark holes where the eyes had been, and that reminded her of the staring eyes and the sermon they seemed to preach to her. Debra was very unhappy.

The following day, Mom came down from the attic looking very serious. "Debra," she called. "I need to talk to you!"

"Yes, Mommy!" Debra answered guiltily. She suspected her mother had seen the damaged painting.

"I was in the attic just now, and I noticed that the painting had holes in it."

"Mommy looks so sad," Debra thought. Tears filled her eyes, and the whole story came out. "I'm so sorry, Mommy," she sobbed. "I wish I never did it!"

"I'm glad to hear you are sorry, but do you see how one sin leads to another?" probed her mother gently. "It started by coveting the spiced apple rings. Then you stole, and because of that you ruined a beautiful painting trying to quiet your conscience. Sin ruins everything—I'm sure those apple rings didn't taste very good, did they?"

"No," admitted Debra. "But worst of all, I just felt so bad inside, in my heart. I don't like that feeling."

"You've apologized to me, dear, and I forgive you, but now you have to ask God for forgiveness,"

her mother said, handing her a tissue. Then she
added seriously, "There's something I want you to
remember, Debra. I have forgiven you, and God will
forgive you when you confess your sin, but remember this: sin can be forgiven, but the effects remain.
What I mean is, all is forgiven, but the painting
remains damaged. Sin always leaves behind a
painful reminder. Sin is destructive, and unpleasant.
But remember this, too, my dear daughter: 'The
blood of Jesus Christ his Son cleanseth us from all
sin.... If we confess our sins, he is faithful and just to
forgive us our sins, and to cleanse us from all
unrighteousness'" (1 John 1:7b, 9).

Debra never forgot the lessons she learned that
day. In His goodness, the Holy Spirit showed Debra
the pain and bitterness of sin, but also the joy of forgiveness. Do you also know this pain and this joy?

—24—
The Conversion of
a "Good Girl"

Not by works of righteousness which we have done, but according to his mercy he saved us, by the washing of regeneration, and renewing of the Holy Ghost.

—Titus 3:5

Miranda was an eighteen-year-old girl, known for her beauty and her sweet character. She had a kind word for everyone, and regularly visited the poor and the sick, always bringing a thoughtful gift with her. Everyone loved her, but she was not pleased with herself.

One evening, at a prayer meeting, her pastor noticed that she seemed troubled. As the meeting progressed, she wept. At the close of the evening, the pastor invited anyone who would like to speak with him to remain behind. Miranda was one of those who stayed.

"Why did you remain behind, Miranda?" asked the minister.

Sobbing, Miranda answered, "My sins!"

Testing her, the minister asked, "But what have

you done which makes you weep? You are such a good girl."

At this, she cried out, "No! I hate God, and I know it! I hate Christians, and I know it! I hate my own being! I wish I had never been born!"

The pastor reminder her that there is forgiveness to be found in Jesus Christ, and that her heart could be renewed by the blood of this Savior. He prayed with her, but Miranda could find no comfort. She felt the weight of her sins. Everyone might think she was a "good girl" but she knew the enmity that lived in her heart. She knew that her sins displeased God, and that made her miserable. She had tried to please God by being "good." She had done her best to be kind to others. But the feeling of guilt deep in her heart would not go away. Now she understood that she could not please God by doing good things. She needed her heart to be cleansed.

On her way out of church, she passed through the library. On a ledge lay a little book called *Village Hymns*. In her desperation to find some comfort, she opened it, and eagerly began to read the first hymn she saw. This is what she read:

> *There is a fountain filled with blood,*
> *Drawn from Immanuel's veins;*
> *And sinners plunged beneath that flood*
> *Lose all their guilty stains.*
>
> *The dying thief rejoiced to see*
> *That fountain in his day;*

And there may I, though vile as he,
Wash all my sins away.

Hope flooded her soul. "This is the answer!" she thought. "This is how I can please God! This is the Savior I need!"

Right there in the library, by the grace of the Holy Spirit, Miranda confessed her sin and found forgiveness with the Lord Jesus Christ. When she got up from her knees, her burden was gone. Her enmity to God was gone. Now she was truly a "good girl," not because of her deeds, but because of Christ's sacrifice.

With tears of thankfulness in her eyes, she read the rest of William Cowper's beautiful hymn.

Dear dying Lamb, Thy precious blood
Shall never lose its power
Till all the ransomed Church of God
Be saved, to sin no more.

E'er since by faith I saw the stream
Thy flowing wounds supply,
Redeeming love has been my theme,
And shall be till I die.

When this poor lisping, stammering tongue
Lies silent in the grave,
Then in a nobler, sweeter song,
I'll sing Thy power to save.

—25—
A Sunday School Student

And that from a child thou hast known the holy scriptures, which are able to make thee wise unto salvation through faith which is in Christ Jesus.
—2 Timothy 3:15

One bright spring morning, a woman entered the poor, dirty home of a family of a little girl named Hannah. Hannah was seven years old and attended Sunday school. She was alone, and was reading so intently that she did not hear the lady's knock, or even hear her open the door. When she called "Hello!" the little girl finally looked up in surprise.

"Oh, good morning, Miss Barton," exclaimed Hannah. "I didn't hear you knock!"

"Good morning, Hannah. Where is your mother?"

"She went to work, and won't be home till supper time."

"Where's Eddie?" asked Miss Barton.

"Mommy took him with her," answered Hannah.

"So there is no one here with you?"

"No, Miss Barton," replied Hannah. "But I don't mind. It gives me time to read."

"What are you reading?" asked Miss Barton, changing the subject.

"I've been learning my texts for next Sunday. I was just reading about Jesus saying, 'Suffer little children to come unto me'" (Matthew 19:14; Mark 10:14; Luke 18:16).

"Why did you choose that passage, Hannah?" questioned Miss Barton.

"Because last night when I tried to teach my little brother again to kneel down with me and say his prayers, Daddy told me I was not allowed to teach him. You know how those bad men made my dad forget about God, don't you?"

"Yes, dear," responded Miss Barton kindly. "What did you say to your father?"

"I said, 'Daddy, Jesus Christ says, "Suffer little children, and forbid them not, to come unto me."'"

"What did your father say then?" Miss Barton was amazed at the wisdom of this child.

"Nothing, but he looked very sad. Then I made Eddie say the Lord's prayer with me."

Miss Barton smiled. "I'm glad. We must pray for your brother, and for your parents, too."

Miss Barton and Hannah visited a while longer. Then Miss Barton asked, "Hannah, are you really okay on your own all day?"

Immediately, with sparkling eyes, Hannah replied, "But Miss Barton, I'm not alone! You know that God is with me!"

What a simple, child-like trust Hannah had!

Hannah continued to attend Sunday school. Miss Barton visited many times, speaking with Hannah's parents as well. The Lord blessed these efforts, along with the many prayers on their behalf. After several months, Hannah's family began to attend church services. The Lord converted Hannah's parents, and Hannah's father was no longer influenced by the men who had called themselves friends. They found far better friends among God's children, and discovered the reward of serving the Lord.

—26—
Torn in Half

Good and upright is the LORD:
therefore will he teach sinners in the way.
—Psalm 25:8

In France many years ago, a peddler greeted a woman living in a forest cottage, and asked her if she would like to buy a New Testament. The woman, named Jeanne, hesitated. Would her husband approve? Wistfully, she eyed the little book, and at last, went inside and got fifty cents to buy it.

"I can't refuse this lovely Book, Monsieur," she smiled. "Thank you."

A short while later, her husband, Jacques, who was a charcoal burner in the forest, came home. Timidly, Jeanne showed him her Book. Just as she had feared, Jacques was not pleased. He grumbled that she had wasted so much money on a Book.

"Oh, Jacques, please don't be angry with me. Remember, I brought some money with me when we married. Fifty cents is not all that much money for such a nice Book. Besides, the money is just as much mine as yours, since we're married."

So they argued back and forth. Finally, Jacques snatched the Book from her hands, saying, "Give me the Book!"

Holding the Bible in his hands, he went on, "The money is half yours and half mine. Very well, then the Book is half yours and half mine too!" Angrily, Jacques opened the Book and tore it into two pieces. "Here! One half for you and one half for me!"

Several days later, Jacques was sitting in the forest when he suddenly remembered the torn Book. He felt for his half, which he carried in his pocket. He decided to investigate it right away, so he opened it and began to read. His rough hands had divided the New Testament at the 15th chapter of Luke's Gospel, and the first words that were on his half of the book were, "and will say unto him, Father, I have sinned against heaven, and before thee, and am no more worthy to be called thy son: make me as one of thy hired servants" (Luke 15:18b, 19).

These were the first words Jacques read, and, spellbound, he read to the end of the story. Then a number of questions came to his mind. What had the poor lost son done? Why had he left home? Where had he been? What made him want to go back home? The questions kept churning through his mind, but he knew the answer was to be found in the first half of the Book, and that was in the hands of his wife. Pride kept him from asking for her half.

Meanwhile, Jeanne went about her daily duties. In her spare time, however, she would read in her half of the New Testament. The more she read, the more interested she became, for the Lord had begun to work in her heart. When she reached the end of her half of the Book, she read about the prodigal son: his waywardness, his journey, his sin, his misery, the wonderful change in his thoughts, and then the words, "How many hired servants of my father's have bread enough and to spare, and I perish with hunger! I will arise and go to my father" (Luke 15:17b, 18a) and there the story stopped.

Oh, the questions that ran through Jeanne's mind! What happened to the son? Did the father welcome him or not? Jeanne hoped that the father had welcomed the boy home again, but was afraid to ask Jacques for the last part of the story.

One day, Jacques came home especially tired, and ate his supper in silence. At last, he cried out, "Oh, Jeanne, can you forgive me for tearing your Book? I cannot rest until I know the beginning! Would you be so kind as to bring me your part?"

"Oh, Jacques," replied his wife, "the same story is always in my mind, too, but I am missing the ending. Did the Father receive that poor wayward son?"

"Yes, he did," answered Jacques, "but what was the sin that separated them? Come, bring your part and we'll read the whole story together."

Jeanne brought her half and sat beside her husband. Together they read the whole story of the prodigal son, and the Spirit of God, who had been working in both their hearts already, revealed to them the meaning of the story. They understood that they were prodigals, too, who needed to return to God.

That was the first of many Bible readings together by the fireside after supper. The blessed Holy Spirit pointed them to Christ as their Lord, their Savior, their Substitute, and helped them to arise and go to their Father, who welcomed them, and saved them for Jesus' sake.

—27—
"Led by the Spirit of God"

Wherefore he is able also to save them to the uttermost that come unto God by him, seeing he ever liveth to make intercession for them.
—Hebrew 7:25

Matthew Johnson worked in a clothing store in the thriving city of Boston. The store was on the other side of the city, too far for him to walk home every evening, so he lived at Mrs. Dennison's Boarding House. Actually, Matthew was relieved to be away from home. His widowed mother was far too religious for his liking.

In the year 1857, there was a revival. Many people were brought to believe in Jesus Christ. Mrs. Johnson had always prayed for her son, but during this special time she was encouraged to continue to wrestle in prayer for the salvation of her son. When she heard that Rev. Finney was scheduled to preach in the section of Boston where her son lived, she decided to ask her son to go with her to church on the coming Lord's Day.

When Matthew received the invitation by mail, he was not pleased. He loved his mother very much. He also knew that his mother was getting older and he did not want to neglect her. But going to church to listen to one of the "revival preachers" was asking a lot! He never prayed, never used God's name, except in vain. He never went to church, and now his mother wanted him to hear one of these somber preachers. Did his mother know what she was asking? Matthew shook his head. He knew what his mother wanted. She wanted him to be a Christian like herself. That would never happen. Alright, he would go. But he would prove to her it would be no use.

Mrs. Johnson arrived at Mrs. Dennison's Boarding House before Matthew was even out of bed.

"What are you doing here so early, Mother?" asked Matthew groggily, lifting his head when his mother knocked on his bedroom door.

"There's a prayer meeting before the service this morning that I wish to go to. You have plenty of time to get dressed and have breakfast," replied Mrs. Johnson with a smile.

Matthew groaned and rolled over. He was irritated. The night before he had been out till very late. He was tired. He wanted to sleep, not go to a prayer meeting!

He was still in a bad mood when they got to the prayer meeting. The songs of praise and the prayers offered to God did not move him. It made him feel uncomfortable, and that made him angry. After the meeting, one of his mother's friends greeted him and asked him if he had been blessed by the prayers.

Rudely, Matthew responded, "I can't stand these revival meetings!"

The worship service was clear and simple, but Matthew realized that God is real, and that he did not know God at all.

Mrs. Johnson's eyes filled with tears as she said goodbye to Matthew. She did not scold him, but told him she loved him. Matthew felt guilty for his bad behavior, and without thinking, he promised he would go with her to the mid-week prayer meeting.

"I can't believe I said that!" he muttered to himself as he shut the door to his room. "Why did I say a thing like that?"

When Mrs. Johnson arrived at the boarding house on Wednesday evening, Matthew tried his best to be pleasant. He was going to do his best to make up for his rudeness on Sunday. The prayer meeting convinced Matthew that the religion of these people was real and true. He wanted it for himself, he realized with surprise. There was no real joy in the life he led, but in the faces of those around him he saw a peace and joy. He realized for the first time in his life that he was very unhappy. He felt ashamed of himself, his wasted time and talents.

After the service, the minister invited all those who would like to speak with the pastor to do so after the service. Matthew hesitated. The last thing he wanted was to be thought of as a serious Christian! But Mrs. Johnson had noticed that her son had listened carefully during the service, and she whispered, "Just go. It won't hurt to ask Rev. Finney a few questions."

When Rev. Finney led the group that had remained behind into a small room, Matthew wondered if he should just leave. What would his friends say if they knew? When the others knelt for prayer, Matthew felt very uncomfortable and wished he hadn't listened to his mother. But as he knelt with the others, it struck him what he was doing. He was kneeling, a sign of humility, before a holy God. Suddenly, he felt terribly unworthy, and filthy. He was guilty of so much sin! What a hypocrite he was, kneeling before God, pretending he was humble, when he was full of sin. He did not hear a word the others said; he hardly noticed they were there. All he was aware of was his sin: his disobedience, his rebellion against the Almighty God, his anger against this God.

His mother had gone home already, so Matthew returned to his boarding house alone. He was glad to be alone, for his thoughts tumbled one over the other. He couldn't sleep. Back and forth, he paced in his room. How could he have lived so many years unconcerned about God's laws? Was there salvation for someone as rebellious as he had been? Matthew looked for a Bible. He didn't have one, but he did have a book of devotions that Mrs. Dennison had left in his room. He read in it a while, but found no relief. He wished he had someone to tell him what to do. Finally, he tried to pray. He was tempted to give up. Why should God listen to him? But he kept on. What else could he do? He began to believe that God was willing to save him. He did not believe yet that his sins were forgiven, but he did believe that if God were willing to hear him, that He would answer him in His own time.

He went to bed, feeling some comfort in this new thought. The next day, Matthew felt happier. Usually, he was grouchy when he woke up, but this morning he was pleasant, thanking Mrs. Dennison for the good breakfast she had prepared. Instead of cursing and swearing, he asked the man next to him to please not use such language.

After work, he bought a Bible, and went home to begin reading. He opened at Psalm 33, and was ashamed that he had ever thought of the Bible as a boring book. He went to his friend downstairs and exclaimed, "You should listen to this psalm. It's amazing! Let me read it to you."

His friend listened politely, but shrugged his shoulders and returned to his newspaper.

The Holy Spirit taught Matthew all the things necessary for salvation. He wrote many letters to his mother, telling of his spiritual struggles, fears, and joys. He asked her many questions too, and she gladly answered each of these precious letters. Mrs. Johnson rejoiced at the change in her dear son, humbled at the amazing love and power of God! After a time, Matthew went to seminary so that he could obey the Lord's calling to tell the story of Jesus Christ.

What about you, children? Are you like Matthew before he was saved? Or has the Holy Spirit worked the same grace in your heart as He did in Matthew's? If you are still living in rebellion against God, then turn now to Him. Do not delay! "I call heaven and earth to record this day against you, that I have set before you life and death, blessing and cursing: therefore choose life, that both thou and thy seed may live" (Deuteronomy 30:19).

—28—
Afraid to Swear Alone

Thou shalt not take the name of the LORD thy God in vain: for the LORD will not hold him guiltless that taketh his name in vain.

—Exodus 20:7

If people are going to steal, or do other wrong things, they usually wish to be alone so that no one will see them. But it is different with those who curse and swear and use God's name in vain. They like to swear in public and have many people hear them. Sometimes children and teenagers like to swear and use bad language so that others will be impressed. They think it proves that they are brave and courageous. And yet it is true that those who swear the worst are often the greatest cowards.

A Christian businessman was greatly shocked one day when a man came into his office swearing and cursing in a terrible way. He looked at the man for a while, and then said to him, "My friend, I will give you a pocket full of money if you will go into the village churchyard at midnight tonight and swear those same oaths there that you have just spoken here, when you are all alone with God."

The man was surprised. "Agreed," he said. "That's an easy way to make some money!"

"Come back here tomorrow," said the Christian businessman, "and tell me if you did it, and I will give you the money."

At midnight the man started for the graveyard. It was a very dark and dismal night. As he entered the churchyard, not a sound could be heard. All was as still as death. Around him, he could see the reminders that death is real—the tombstones of former villagers cast shadows in the darkness. The church itself seemed to proclaim that God is not dead, as he had tried to tell himself. Then the Christian man's words, "when you are all alone with God" rang in his ears. He began to tremble. He felt that God was right there, close by his side. He was terrified! The idea of cursing and swearing when God seemed nearer than ever, terrified him. He did not

dare to utter a single oath. Instead, he ran home, dashed up the stairs to his bedroom, and fell on his knees by his bed. "God, be merciful to me, a sinner!" he wept. He spent the night wrestling with God, begging for forgiveness of his sins. And God, in His infinite kindness and mercy, forgave also this man.

Never think that your sins are too many for God to wipe away. Do not stay away from the precious Savior, who gladly receives sinners. "If thou, LORD, shouldest mark iniquities, O Lord, who shall stand? But there is forgiveness with thee, that thou mayest be feared" (Psalm 130:3-4).

—29—
The Sailor's Bible

Thy word is a lamp unto my feet, and a light unto my path.
—Psalm 119:105

After returning from a voyage, a sailor visited a shop to buy his wife a gift. He noticed a Bible lying on the counter, and inquired, "What is the title of that book?"

The shopkeeper answered, "That is a Bible, sir. Would you like to buy it?"

"A Bible?" echoed the sailor. "Yes, I would very much like to buy it."

The shopkeeper, knowing that few sailors were educated, asked politely, "If you don't mind my asking, can you read, sir?"

"No, I can't," frowned the sailor, "but it would look very respectable to have a Bible in our house."

The shopkeeper was surprised, but was glad to make a sale. The sailor carried the Bible home, thinking his wife would be delighted with the gift. She couldn't read either, but he was convinced that putting it on the little table near her chair would make quite an impression on anyone who came to visit.

When he presented the Bible to his wife, however, she was not at all pleased. Rather, she was angry.

"Why did you waste your money on something that neither of us can use? You could have bought something useful!" So, instead of being a source of pride, the Bible was a source of strife between them. It did not rest on the little table by the woman's chair, but in a drawer in the spare room.

Soon after this, two men from a Bible Society knocked on the door. They asked the sailor's wife if she would like to support the Bible Society, or buy a Bible. The very mention of the word "Bible" reminded her of her husband's gift to her, and she angrily informed the men that she already had a Bible which neither she nor her husband could read. The men talked to her about the value of the Bible and how much wisdom was to be found in its pages. Thinking the men were talking only of its material value, the woman became interested. Perhaps her husband hadn't been so foolish after all, she thought. The men urged her to attend a local school which offered classes teaching adults to read. She promised the men she would do so.

It was not long before the sailor's wife was reading without much difficulty. Proudly, she read aloud a chapter every evening to her husband. The sailor was so impressed that he decided he would also attend the reading classes. He, too, quickly learned to read.

As you know, simply reading the Bible is not enough for salvation. But the Holy Spirit blessed these evening readings to the hearts of both the sailor and his wife. They began to understand that the men from the Bible Society were not talking about the outward value of the Bible, but its eternal value. The Holy Spirit began to teach them the truths found in the pages of God's Word.

The sailor and his wife began to go to church, and there they learned more about themselves and about God. Most importantly, they learned about the Lord Jesus Christ who calls sinners to Himself. How ashamed they were to think that they had only wanted a Bible to look respectable! How glad they were that they had been taught by the Holy Spirit what the Bible says!

Do you know what the Bible says? Do you believe that the Bible speaks the truth? Have you repented of your sin? Do you love to read the Bible? To be able to read the Bible is a great blessing, but it is a greater blessing to be taught God's Word by the Holy Spirit. "Search the scriptures; for in them ye think ye have eternal life: and they are they which testify of me" (John 5:39).

—30—
"What if it Had Been You?"

Be ye therefore ready also: for the Son of man cometh at an hour when ye think not.

—Luke 12:40

When Edward Brown was about ten years old, an event occurred in the village where he lived, which he never forgot. Perhaps it will be something you will never forget either. Among the children of the village was a little girl named Alice, about four years of age. If you would have passed by her house on a bright spring morning, you would have seen her playing in her yard, picking dandelions, talking to her doll, or watching the robins eat their breakfast.

Alice had learned from her earliest days to love the Savior. Young as she was, she knew her heart was sinful and needed to be renewed. She loved to hear the Bible stories, and tried her best to learn Bible texts, and songs about the Lord. When people came to visit her parents, she would talk to them in her childish way about the Lord Jesus, the friend of children.

Across the far side of the garden ran a beautiful stream of water. It was pleasant to look at as it hurried along, with the garden flowers bending over it.

Little Alice sometimes played near the garden, but was never left there alone, as her parents were afraid she might fall into the stream. It was not very deep, hardly waist high, but enough to cover her should she fall down.

One morning, Alice had slipped unnoticed into the garden, and, not realizing the danger, began to play along the bank of the stream. Happily, she picked flowers, and watched the stream bubble merrily on its way, when suddenly her foot slipped, and she fell. No one heard her cry. There could have been only a short struggle in the fast-moving stream, and then it was over. They found her soon after, lying face-down in the water. Gently, they lifted her out of the stream, and smoothed back the wet hair from the precious little face. There was no doubt that one more little lamb had gone home to the Good Shepherd, and they knew that the voice which would no more be heard on earth was already mingling with the joyful voices of the redeemed in heaven.

The sad story of Alice's drowning spread like wildfire though the village. Edward Brown soon heard it, and with a grieving heart he ran home to tell his mother.

"Yes, my son, I have heard all about it," she answered, with trembling voice and tearful eyes. "Dear little Alice has been taken home by her Savior. She loved to sing and speak about Him for her heart was full of Him. There's no question that she is rejoicing with the angels in heaven. But Edward," she added solemnly, turning to look her son full in the face, "what if it had been you?"

That was all Edward's mother said to him that day about little Alice. Edward grew up, got a job, married, and had children, but he never forgot his mother's earnest question all those years before. It went straight to his heart, and the Holy Spirit used that question to awaken him to the reality of death and life after death. From the day his mother asked that solemn question, Edward thought seriously about his soul. Anxious thought filled his heart. Was he prepared to meet God? What if it had been he who had died that day? The Holy Spirit led Edward to see the wickedness of his heart, but also to experience the forgiveness found only through the blood of the Lord Jesus Christ. He has often told his children the story of Alice, and asks them the same question his mother asked him all those years before, "What if it had been you?"

—31—
An Unexpected Change

*And let us not be weary in well doing: for in due season
we shall reap, if we faint not.*   —Galatians 6:9

*This story was written by a minister who lived in America
in the colonial days.*

For the first eighteen years of my ministry I pastored
a country village, which was surrounded by several
family farms. Within a mile and a half of the parson-
age lived Mr. and Mrs. Blythe and their children.
Mr. Blythe grew up during a time when few schools
were found in the county, and he could neither read
nor write. He had always been a good husband and
father, a hard worker, providing a comfortable home
for his family. Although the Blythes regularly
attended church, they did not seem to understand
the need for salvation. I felt great concern for this
family, and often visited them, trying to explain the
simplest truths of Scripture to them. I prayed that
the Holy Spirit would open their eyes to see their
need of a Savior. All my prayers and efforts, however, seemed to be in vain. Both Mr. and Mrs.

Blythe seemed content with their lives, and felt no need to seek the Lord. I visited them less and less often, so that I could give my time to others who were more ready to receive the truth.

One evening, when I was slowly making my way home on horseback through the pine forest which surrounded the Blythe farm, I wondered if I should visit the Blythes again. I wanted to try once more to awaken them from their sleep of death. They were at home when I arrived and welcomed me into their home. I soon stated the purpose of my visit, warning them of the danger of putting off repentance and salvation. To my surprise, however, instead of showing the usual lack of interest in what I was saying, I was delighted to see that Mr. and Mrs. Blythe showed great concern for their souls. They were filled with sorrow for ignoring God's warnings for so many years. They asked, "What must we do to be saved?"

My heart overflowed with joy and gratitude to

God for His mercy. In my blindness, I had thought these people were hardened beyond hope. With humble thanksgiving in my heart, I read and explained the Scriptures, and prayed with them.

Just before I left, I asked them, "Is there a particular incident or event that caused you to begin feeling concern for your souls? What was the turning point?"

They told me that their children had attended a Sunday school in town for two years. On Sunday afternoons, the older children would take turns reading the Bible and Christian children's books aloud to the younger children. This simple means of grace had reached their hearts. They had been led by the Holy Spirit to see that they were sinners, and lost without the Lord Jesus Christ. Now they wanted to know if and how they could find grace and mercy with God. Of course, I gladly explained once again the wonderful story of Christ's sacrifice for sinners.

After this, I visited them often, and rejoiced to see them growing in grace with their children. They became members of the church, and were a blessing to many, both in the church and in their community.

Never assume that the time of grace is past for anyone. Also, never let Satan deceive you into thinking that you have sinned too much or too long for the Lord to save you. The Lord can reach the hardest hearts. He delights in mercy (Micah 7:18). "For thy mercy is great above the heavens: and thy truth reacheth unto the clouds" (Psalm 108:4).

—32—
The Good One Bible Did

The entrance of thy words giveth light; it giveth understanding to the simple.   —Psalm 119:130

A Roman Catholic woman had been ill for several weeks, and was feeling down. One day, while wandering through the streets of London, she passed by a theater. Seeing that the door was open, and that people were going inside, she supposed that a play was being performed and decided to go in and see it. But she had only been seated a few minutes when she heard someone say, "Let us pray."

A city missionary had rented the building for the purpose of holding a worship service. When the lady realized her mistake, she stood up to leave, but in doing so, she dropped her purse and her umbrella. This made so much noise in the quiet building that everyone turned and looked at her. So she thought it best to quietly sit down again and listen to the minister. The words she heard had a powerful effect on her. She saw that she was a lost sinner, without a saving knowledge of the Lord Jesus Christ.

When the service was over, she approached the minister and asked if she could speak with him. She told him of the burden of sin that was pressing upon her, and asked how she could find relief.

"I have a cure for you," answered the minister. "Take this book and read it." He handed her his

pocket Bible. "I am sure it will show you what to do with your sins, and you will find what you seek."

She took the book and promised to read it. She did so, and by the Spirit's grace, the reading of it made a great change in her. It led her to know and love the Savior, as she had never done before. The burden of her sins was taken away, and this made her very happy.

She stopped going to the Roman Catholic church. Before long, the priest, who was a kind friend of hers, came to see her to find out why she had not been coming to church. She showed him the book she had been reading, and told him what a wonderful change it had made in her by the saving work of the Holy Spirit. "I never knew how sin had separated me from God and what God has provided in Jesus Christ to reconcile sinners to Himself."

Then she gave the book to the priest, and asked him to read it too, and tell her what he thought of it. The priest took the book and read it. The reading of it led to a change in him, just like it had changed the lady. The Holy Spirit opened his eyes too, and he received a new heart.

Not long after this, the priest became very ill, and died suddenly. But the knowledge of Jesus Christ as his Savior had taken away all fear of death and he died in peace.

During his sickness one of the nuns who took care of him became very interested in the Bible the priest was reading. He told her all about it, and how much he had learned from it. He told her about the Lord Jesus, the Lamb of God, who came to take away the sins of the world out of free grace alone.

After the priest's death, the nun noticed the Bible on the priest's desk as she was cleaning out his room. Thinking about the powerful effect it had had on the priest, she took it with her. She wanted to read it for herself. So she carried it to her room and read it carefully. The Holy Spirit also blessed this woman and she too received a new heart. She learned the truth in Jesus, as she had never known it before, and she became a child of God.

In this way the Lord used a Bible, His precious Word, to draw three sinners to Himself. In a very simple way, these people came to know the Lord Jesus. The Word of God is simple but powerful when applied by the Holy Spirit. Have you been renewed by the work of the Holy Spirit? Have your sins been washed away in the blood of Jesus? Do you love to read the Bible?

—33—
Prayers for Salvation

So then every one of us shall give account of himself to God.
—Romans 14:12

There was once a girl, whom we will name Deborah, who had godly parents. They loved their daughter very much, and desired her salvation. They prayed constantly for her. Though they made every effort to make sure she was well clothed, fed, and educated, their main concern was that she be saved. Deborah knew this, and she came to a very wrong conclusion. She decided that because her parents loved her so much, and prayed every day for her salvation, she didn't need to pray for herself. She thought, "God loves my father and mother very much, and certainly He will hear their prayers. I don't have to pray for myself, because their prayers are good enough. I will never be lost, since so many prayers are offered to God on my behalf by such godly parents." It was not that she did not want to be saved—she did, or so she thought. But she forgot that no one can earn salvation for another person. She felt quite safe simply because her parents prayed for her. The Holy Spirit often touched her conscience, but she reasoned that she didn't have to beg for mercy or wrestle in prayer, because her parents did it for her.

God, in His loving mercy and great patience, saw the danger Deborah was in. He did something that did not *seem* loving: he took away her beloved mother. From that moment, Deborah later said, she felt as though half her dependence was gone, but still, she leaned upon her father's prayers. She believed her father could be her intercessor. Then, again, God did something for Deborah that did not seem loving: her father became sick, and after a time of illness, he died. At last, Deborah felt that every prop was removed. She had no one left to pray for her! She had no one to depend on! Her father was not yet buried. He lay in the coffin. No longer could he pray for his daughter. Deborah was filled with panic. Who would pray for her? She was alone, unprotected! Now, finally, she saw her danger. Falling down on her knees, she cried out to God, "Lord, save me, or I perish!" She told the Lord that she did not dare to get up from her knees until He

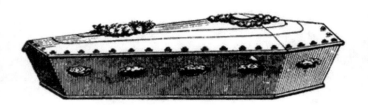

saved her. How long she stayed on her knees she did not know, but the Lord graciously heard Deborah's prayers.

Was it Deborah's prayer that saved her? No. May we not pray for one another? Yes, we must! But God had to teach Deborah that her parents could not save her. It is God who saves; it is Jesus Christ who intercedes; it is the Holy Spirit who teaches us to cry out to Him. When the Lord taught Deborah this, she cried out to Him, and then the Lord was pleased to answer her prayers.

Do you pray? Or, are you like Deborah, foolishly thinking that your parents' or grandparents' prayers are good enough for you? Do you make the mistake of thinking that God will save you because you have godly ancestors? While it is a blessing to have godly parents and family members who pray for you, you must never build your hopes on this like Deborah did. Go to God in prayer and ask Him to make you one of His dear children.

—34—
The Watchword

Unto you therefore which believe he is precious.
—1 Peter 2:7a

In one of the great rock passageways of the fortress
of Gibraltar, two British soldiers were assigned as
midnight guards at each end of a long tunnel in the
fortress. One of them was a happy Christian, rejoicing in the peace which he had found in Jesus. The
other was distressed with the burden of his sins. He
had, for a long time, felt the need of a Savior, but he
had never come to Jesus, and was a stranger to "the
peace of God, which passeth all understanding"
(Philippians 4:7a).

In the silence of the night these soldiers were
doing their rounds. One of them was meditating on
the atoning blood of Christ, which had brought peace
to his soul. The other was groaning under the burden
of his sins, and longing to be rid of that burden.

Suddenly, an officer came in sight. In passing
the first sentinel, the officer paused, and asked for
the watchword. The startled soldier, forgetting for
the moment what the watchword was, and thinking
only of the peace that filled his soul and of the

source from which it came, exclaimed, "The precious blood of Christ!" (1 Peter 1:19). Then, correcting himself, he gave the real watchword, and the officer passed on, greatly wondering, no doubt, at the soldier's words.

But those words the soldier had spoken rang through the tunnel, and reached the ears of the soldier posted at the other end. They entered his heart, and it seemed to him as if an angel from heaven had sent him this message: "The precious blood of Christ!" He knew this was what he needed. In penitence and faith he turned to Jesus. His burden rolled off at the foot of the cross, and his soul found rest.

—35—
Songs in the Night

Labor not for the meat which perisheth, but for that meat which endureth unto everlasting life, which the Son of man shall give unto you: for him hath God the Father sealed.

—John 6:27

Emily Rushton was one of many young men and women who attended college in Washington. She was not only a good student, but friendly and well-liked. Soon after she began her studies, Emily realized that hard work was rewarded with good grades. She determined to do her very best to get top grades. Every day she studied for hours, but she neglected the most important book, the Bible. When she had packed for college, her Bible went into the suitcase, but as Emily became more and more determined to get the best grades, she skipped her devotions more often than not. Increasingly, she neglected to pray, and then her church attendance began to slip as well.

Exams were approaching, and Emily studied harder than ever. She got up before dawn, and studied before classes began. She studied while she ate, and far into the night. Her friends tried to encourage her to put her books aside for a while, to get some fresh air, or to visit some friends together, but Emily refused.

Such intense study took its toll. One afternoon about two weeks before exams, Emily felt hot and sleepy. She tried hard to keep her eyes open as she sat at her desk at school. After a little while, she began to shiver. She was so cold! Her joints ached, and she wanted to go back to bed.

When she arrived at her dorm room, Emily's room mate, Judy, looked at her with concern. "Emily, you're sick!"

"No, I'm not," responded Emily stubbornly. "I'm just cold."

Judy threw up her hands in frustration. "Emily, you've been studying way too hard! You've worn yourself out, and now you're sick! I'm going to put you to bed!"

Emily was too tired to resist. She was actually grateful to be put to bed. Perhaps if she had a nap she could study some more. After she had slept for a while, Emily dragged herself to her desk and began to study. Exams were coming up, she told herself. She had to study! When she was exhausted she went back to bed for a while before getting up to do the same thing again.

Emily was losing weight. She was pale and thin. Sometimes the fever would leave for a while when she took some aspirin, but always it would return. When Judy discovered Emily unconscious on the

floor one evening, she frantically called an ambulance and Emily was taken to the hospital.

Judy called Emily's family who came as soon as they could. Instead of getting better, it seemed Emily was getting worse. The doctors told the Rushtons that Emily was very sick, and that they needed to do more tests. Emily's ten-year-old sister Ruth had come along too. She insisted on sitting beside Emily's bedside. One night, Ruth sat quietly by Emily's beside. She cried softly when she looked at her sister's thin, pale face, and watched her toss and turn.

"If only there was something I could do for you, Emily!" cried Ruth.

"I keep thinking that exams start tomorrow, and I won't be able to do them. Can you sing to me, to get my mind off it?" asked Emily.

Ruth didn't think she could manage to sing, but she asked, "What would you like me to sing?"

"It doesn't matter, Ruth. Anything."

Softly Ruth began to sing one of the songs she had recently learned in Sunday School.

> *Depth of mercy! Can there be*
> *Mercy still reserved for me?*
> *Can my God His wrath forbear—*
> *Me, the chief of sinners, spare?*
>
> *I have long withstood His grace,*
> *Long provoked Him to His face,*
> *Would not hearken to His calls,*
> *Grieved Him by a thousand falls.*
>
> *Now incline me to repent,*
> *Let me now my sins lament,*
> *Now my foul revolt deplore,*
> *Weep, believe, and sin no more.*
>
> *There for me my Savior stands,*
> *Holding forth His wounded hands;*
> *God is love! I know, I feel,*
> *Jesus weeps and loves me still.*[1]

Quietly, Ruth sang, unaware of the impact the words had on her sister's heart. Emily listened, seeming to hear the familiar song for the first time in her life. The Holy Spirit used these words to convict Emily of what she was missing. Tears coursed down her fevered cheeks as she felt the pain and guilt of her sin of wandering far away from God.

Ruth noticed the tears on her sister's face, and noticed her troubled expressions. Eager to comfort Emily, Ruth sang another familiar hymn.

Rock of ages, cleft for me,
Let me hide myself in Thee;
Let the water and the blood,
From Thy wounded side which flowed,
Be of sin the double cure,
Save from wrath and make me pure.

In my hand no price I bring;
Simply to Thy cross I cling;
Could my tears forever flow,
Could my zeal no languor know,
These for sin could not atone;
Thou must save, and Thou alone.[2]

Ruth sang more songs, and they soothed Emily's soul. For the first time in many days, Emily slept peacefully. This marked the turning point in her illness, and in her life. The Holy Spirit used the songs Ruth sang for Emily's conversion. She saw her sin in making an idol of her studies. Her schoolwork had become more important than God. She was ashamed of neglecting Him. When she acknowledged her sin, these solemn songs in the night not only soothed Emily's mind, but her heart found peace with God.

After Emily was well again, she finished her studies. She was not at the top of her class, but she knew she had done her best. She learned that her focus must be the honor and glory of God. Through her suffering she was taught the right perspective. Her prayer became, "Lord, use me in Thy kingdom." Wherever she went, Emily did what she could to help others. She talked to people about the Lord Jesus Christ, the only way of salvation, and she helped those in need. By her witness, many people were led to know the Lord Jesus. She often repeated the text, "It is good for me that I have been afflicted; that I might learn thy statutes" (Psalm 119:71). Are you learning the lessons that God is giving you?

---

[1]Charles Wesley, 1707-1788
[2]Augustus M. Toplady, 1740-1778

—36—
The Siberian Leper

And if thou draw out thy soul to the hungry, and satisfy the afflicted soul; then shall thy light rise in obscurity, and thy darkness be as the noonday.

—Isaiah 58:10

Siberia is a very cold country. It is also very large: more than three thousand, six hundred miles long, and nearly two thousand miles wide. It is not a very easy place to live in, since the ground is mostly covered with snow, and the rivers are frozen over for more than half a year. Few flowers are found in the land, and the trees bear little fruit. Most of the year, it is like a frozen desert.

Long ago, there was a tribe of people living in Siberia called the Tartars, or the Tatars. They would rarely settle in towns, but wandered about from place to place, living in tents. Most of these Tatars worshipped the false prophet Mohammed or a Buddhist monk named Lama. They also bowed before gods of wood and stone made by their own hands.

Missionaries sent to Siberia attempted to teach the Tatars about the true God of heaven and earth, and His only Son, the Lord Jesus Christ. God blessed the work of these missionaries, and some of these people became Christians. One day a missionary approached a group of Tatar tents, when he saw a man lying on the ground, nearly dead. He was a leper. Leprosy is a sad disease: the body is covered with large white sores; slowly, the body wastes away. Almost always, the leper was shunned, since there were no hospitals willing to treat him, and his own family turned from him in disgust. This leper, too, was left to perish alone.

When Jesus lived on earth, He had pity on lepers. Love to Christ leads His people to feel compassion for suffering people, too. Now, when the missionary saw this poor leper, he wanted to help him. The man looked up at the missionary as he approached, and a look of joy came over his face. "I know you," he cried.

"How can that be?" asked the missionary, thoroughly surprised. "Have you seen me before?"

"Yes, I have," replied the dying man eagerly. "Didn't you preach in a marketplace once in the big city?"

"I could have, but I don't remember," answered the missionary.

"Don't you remember standing on the steps of a house, preaching to some people?" prodded the man.

"Yes, I think I remember it now," smiled the missionary.

"You told us about Jesus who died to save

sinners," said the leper. "You said that men of every nation may come to Him, and that He would receive and save them. O, sir, I never heard such wonderful things before. I believed in Him that day. He is my Savior, and soon I will be with Him forever. I am dying. No one will help me now, but I have Jesus. That is enough."

Touched by what he had heard and seen, the missionary went into one of the tents nearby, where he found several Tatars drinking. He asked them, "Why do you not go to your brother? He lies there dying with nobody to help him!"

"Brother!" they sneered, "He is no brother of ours! He is a dog!"

Again, the missionary tried to move these men to feel some pity for their fellow Tatar, but they refused to help. So the missionary went back to the poor leper, to try to comfort him. Not long afterward, the man died. Since there was no one to bury him, the missionary dug a grave, and gently placed the diseased body of the poor leper into the ground. There he will lie till the great judgment day, when the Lord will give him a new body to glorify Him forever.

With tears of joy, the missionary thanked the Lord for allowing him to be with the leper as he died. He marveled how the Lord planned this for the poor Siberian leper. Rejected by his family and friends, God brought a fellow Christian to his side to comfort him in his last moments, and bury him after he died. The missionary went on his way, rejoicing at God's mercy, thanking Him that the poor Siberian leper was now in heaven, and would not have to suffer any more disease and neglect. "And God shall wipe away all tears from their eyes; and there shall be no more death, neither sorrow, nor crying, neither shall there be any more pain: for the former things are passed away" (Revelation 21:4).

—37—
Rebecca's Refuge

In God is my salvation, my glory: the rock of my strength, and my refuge, is in God. Trust in him at all times; ye people, pour out your heart before him: God is a refuge for us. Selah.

—Psalm 62:7, 8

"If I am not better tomorrow, you must write to your uncle James," Mrs. Ferguson said to her daughter Rebecca.

Rebecca leaned over her mother and wiped her forehead. She knew her mother would not be better tomorrow. "I'll write again today, mother," she promised.

"It won't be any use, I'm afraid," admitted Mrs. Ferguson. "I've written so often in vain, that I told myself I wouldn't try again. But I don't know what else to do. James is my only brother, twelve years older than I am. I haven't seen him for almost twenty years. He was angry with me for marrying your father. He told me then that he never wanted to see me again, and I'm afraid he means to keep his word. I just hope that he will have pity on you after I die."

"You must not worry, mother dear," soothed

Rebecca, although she herself was already fretting about her future.

Mrs. Ferguson died unexpectedly a few days later. Sixteen-year-old Rebecca was now an orphan. Kind neighbors attended the funeral, and helped Rebecca pack her belongings. She could not stay in the little cottage that had been her home for so long, because Rebecca did not have money to pay for the rent.

Rebecca had not been taught to pray. She had no idea what to do or where to go. But God provided for this poor orphan girl. One of the neighbors offered that Rebecca come to live with them. Gladly, she accepted, and made herself as useful as she could in her new home.

It soon became clear, however, that these kind

people could not afford to keep Rebecca any longer. For a few months she found work with the village seamstress, but after the busyness of spring was past, the seamstress told Rebecca she didn't need her anymore.

"Why don't you go into the big city and look for a job there?" suggested the seamstress. "Look up Mr. Brunson. He owns a shop that sells clothing. Most likely he could use you."

Having no other choice, Rebecca walked the forty miles to the city, and found Mr. Brunson's shop. He was indeed willing to hire her, much to Rebecca's relief. But when Rebecca started her search for a room to rent, she found that the wages Mr. Brunson offered to pay her would not be able to get her a decent room. She was very anxious and frightened. She was an orphan, all alone in a big city, with no friends.

When she told her new employer her problem, he asked kindly, "Don't you have any friends or family in the city?"

"Well, my uncle James lives here, but I've never seen him. I really don't think he'll want anything to do with me," answered Rebecca sadly.

"You could at least try," encouraged Mr. Brunson. "Let's find his address, and then you can pay him a visit. Cheer up," he added, seeing Rebecca's worried look, "it will all work out."

Taking with her the address Mr. Brunson had

copied for her onto a scrap of paper, a tiny photo of
her mother, and a ring her uncle James had given
her mother when she was a girl, Rebecca set out to
find her uncle. Her heart pounded and her mouth
felt dry.

When she knocked, a servant answered the door
and led her into the parlor. After a few minutes her
Uncle James and Aunt Margaret came in. It was just
as she feared. Uncle James looked like a gruff,
unhappy man. Aunt Margaret, however, was a timid,
quiet woman, who greeted Rebecca kindly.

Rebecca told her story, and showed her uncle
the ring and the photo. He studied the picture of his
sister silently for a few moments, then looked at
Rebecca and sighed.

"Yes, that's my sister," he stated. He frowned. "But
that doesn't mean that we'll let you stay with us."

"But James," argued Aunt Margaret bravely.
"She has nowhere else to go!"

For a moment, Uncle James looked surprised
that his wife would dare to oppose him, but after a
pause, he gave in. "I suppose we have no choice but
to take you in."

When Uncle James left the room, Aunt Margaret smiled and hugged Rebecca. "I've always
wanted a child," she whispered. "Now I have you!"

So God provided a job and a home for Rebecca.

It turned out, also in Gods providence, that Mr.
Brunson was the best employer Rebecca could have

had, for he was a child of God. He truly cared about the souls of the young ladies working for him, and soon discovered that even though Rebecca was a pleasant, well-mannered young lady, she was not a Christian.

During this time, God was visiting some of the city churches with a revival, and services were held several evenings a week. Mr. Brunson urged the young ladies working for him to attend these meetings. Normally Rebecca and the others worked during the evening as well, but Mr. Brunson told them that if they wanted to attend the church services, he would give them the time off.

At first Rebecca did not go with the other girls to the meetings. She would rather work and earn money. "What if I lose my job, or what if Uncle James changes his mind?" she worried.

Jane, one of the seamstresses who worked with Rebecca, had been attending as many meetings as she could, and the Holy Spirit had begun working in her heart. "Come with us, Rebecca," urged Jane the following evening.

"Alright, just this once then," agreed Rebecca reluctantly. She had to admit that a break from work would be good for her.

For the first time in her life, Rebecca heard the truth as it is in Christ Jesus. When Mrs. Ferguson had been healthy, she had occasionally taken Rebecca to church, but it was a church which did not teach the full truth. Church attendance, religion, Bible reading, and God were not considered important in Rebecca's family. When Rebecca moved in with her uncle and aunt, she was anxious to please especially her Uncle James. Every Sunday, Rebecca would read to him, do some accounting for his business, and take a walk with him. Now, in church, under the Holy Spirit's influence, Rebecca's eyes were opened, and she saw that she was a sinner, guilty before a holy God. "What must I do to be saved?" was the question which filled her heart. She was agitated, distracted, and sad. Seeing this, Jane urged her to come with her the following evening as well. "Perhaps you'll find the answers you need," encouraged Jane. "I'll pray for you."

Again, Rebecca went to God's house, and again, she heard the way of salvation explained. This time the Holy Spirit showed her that Jesus Christ had made atonement for her sins, and that eternal life was freely offered to her. She was urged to repent of her sins and go to the Savior for healing and forgiveness. Humbly and joyfully, Rebecca asked the Lord Jesus to wash away her sins and to give her a new heart. Soon, she was enabled to rejoice in Him as "the way, the truth, and the life" (John 14:6).

When Rebecca returned home, she told her aunt and uncle about her new-found joy in the Lord Jesus. Her uncle was not pleased. Rebecca had expected this, but it made her sad. She resolved to pray for both her uncle and her aunt.

When Rebecca came downstairs the following Sunday dressed for church, her uncle asked her, "Where do you think you're going?"

"I'd like to go to church with my friend Jane," answered Rebecca.

"You are not going to that church!" shouted Uncle James. "They're a bunch of religious fanatics. You stay away from them, do you hear?"

A knock sounded on the door, and Rebecca's heart began to pound. "That's probably Jane," Rebecca said softly.

Angrily, Uncle James strode to the door. There stood Jane, her Bible in her hands. "Rebecca is not going to church with you," he said roughly. "And don't come here again." He closed the door in her face.

Crying, Rebecca left the room and went upstairs. If she was not allowed to go to church, at least she could read the Bible Mr. Brunson had lent her. She had just begun to read when a servant knocked on the door. "Your uncle wishes to see you downstairs, Miss Rebecca."

With a prayer, Rebecca went back downstairs. Her uncle sat in the living room. "I want you to do that accounting for me," he ordered harshly.

Rebecca sat down at the desk. She wanted to make her uncle happy. But then she remembered that the Ten Commandments teach us that we may not work on the Lord's Day. She put down her pen and found her aunt in the kitchen.

"Aunt Margaret, Uncle James asked me to do his accounting, and I may not. It's Sunday," whispered Rebecca. "Would you go and talk to him for me, please?"

But Aunt Margaret was too timid. "He'll be so angry. Why don't you just do as he asks?"

Rebecca shook her head. "I can't. It's against God's law. I'd rather offend Uncle James than offend God."

Aunt Margaret shook her head sadly as Rebecca went to find Uncle James.

"Oh, God, please help me," prayed Rebecca.

She returned to the living room. "Uncle James, I cannot do as you ask. I'm sorry."

He was furious. He called her names. He told her she thought she was better than others. He accused her of being ungrateful and disrespectful. Rebecca cried, offering to do anything for him but break the Sabbath, but it was no use. Every time she spoke, he became angrier. "If you don't quit that religion of yours, you'll have to leave! Go to your room, and tomorrow morning you can tell me what you've decided."

Heartbroken, the girl returned to her bedroom. What should she do? Was she really being disrespectful? But if she did as her uncle requested, she would be disobeying her Lord and Savior, and she dared not do that. Hadn't He said, "Whosoever shall deny me before men, him will I also deny before my Father which is in heaven" (Matthew 10:33)? Eagerly, Rebecca read her Bible, beseeching her heavenly Father to show her the right path and to give her the grace and strength to follow it, regardless of the outcome. All day she prayed and read, and by evening "the peace of God which passeth all understanding" (Philippians 4:7) filled her heart. Trustingly she committed her way to Him, and slept peacefully.

When she awoke, she dressed and went downstairs. She felt calm, for she knew God was with her. Expecting to see an angry, cold hearted man, she was surprised to see Uncle James pacing the floor. He seemed frantic with worry. Before Rebecca could ask what was the matter, he groaned, "Rebecca, Rebecca, tell me what to do! I'm an awful sinner! Pray for me, if you will!"

Rebecca was so amazed at this drastic change in her uncle that she couldn't think of anything to say. Uncle James looked at her and explained, "Yesterday I felt terrible after I'd shouted at you. My conscience kept bothering me, and I couldn't concentrate on anything. Your Aunt Margaret must have noticed, because she found a Bible and suggested we find out what it is that makes you so strong. Every chapter she read to me made me feel worse. I am such a sinner! Rebecca, will you please help me?"

Quickly getting over her surprise, Rebecca

agreed to pray with her uncle. In a faltering voice, she asked the Lord to show Uncle James the way to the Savior so that he could find peace for his soul. Not knowing much about her new Lord, Rebecca offered to get Mr. Brunson, who, of course, was delighted to visit Rebecca's uncle and aunt. He spoke to them about the Lord Jesus Christ, the only Way of salvation. His simple words were blessed to their hearts, and they also found the refuge their niece had discovered: the Lord Jesus Christ.

—38—
The Mathematician Confounded

Wherefore do ye spend money for that which is not bread? and your labor for that which satisfieth not? Hearken diligently unto me, and eat ye that which is good, and let your soul delight itself in fatness.

—Isaiah 55:2

At one of the first colleges in America, a young man had graduated and was honored for his achievements, especially his knowledge of mathematics. This young man found a good job, and settled in a town where a faithful minister of the gospel also labored.

It was not long before the minister met him on one of his evening walks, and after they had talked awhile, the minister understood that the young man was not in any way religious. Rather, the man had dreams of becoming rich and famous, living only for this world.

Praying for wisdom, the pastor spoke up as they were about to part ways. "I have heard that you are noted for your mathematical skill. I have a problem which I would like you to solve."

"What is it?" the young man inquired eagerly.

The minister answered, looking compassionately at the young man, "'What shall it profit a man, if he shall gain the whole world, and lose his own soul?'"

The young man was speechless. He had not expected a question like this! He returned home, and tried to shake off the impression of this burning question, but he could not. He tried to drown it by going to parties, by studying harder, and by working late into the night, but the question remained: "What shall it profit a man, if he shall gain the whole world, and lose his own soul?"

Thankfully, the young man did not continue to resist the Spirit's knocking, but by God's grace he yielded, and was saved. Later, he became a minister and defended the same gospel which he had once disdained.

—39—
The Hour Alone with God

All scripture is given by inspiration of God, and is profitable for doctrine, for reproof, for correction, for instruction in righteousness.

—2 Timothy 3:16

A godly father had an ungodly son. The father had raised him in the fear of the Lord, reading the Bible to him often, praying and talking with him, but in spite of his father's faithful teachings, John turned his back on the Lord. He hardened his heart against his father's gentle pleadings, stern warnings, and tearful prayers. He chose friends who led him further into sin, and who did not care that they sinned against God.

At last John's father became ill. John came to see his father, for though he did not obey him, he did love him. Before he died, John's father asked him, "My son, would you promise me something? It would ease my suffering and give me some comfort."

Hesitantly, John agreed. "What do you want me to do, Father?"

"Just this, dear son. Will you promise me, that after I die you will spend an hour alone in your room every day?"

"That's it?" John asked in surprise. "What do you want me to do there? I suppose you want me to pray or read the Bible or something."

"Just an hour alone in your room," repeated his father weakly.

John thought it was a very strange request, but was relieved that he didn't have to promise to do anything religious. "I promise to do that for you, Father. You've been so good to me; that will be easy enough to do for you."

Not long after this, the father died. John kept his promise, determined to keep his word. He knew he had caused his father much grief, and wanted to do at least this much for him. An hour alone in his room: what was he going to do during that hour? At first, he spent the time straightening out his room. He found some books his father had given him, but he did not want to read them. He put them back on the shelf. Another time he played cards by himself, but he soon tired of that. Sometimes he fell asleep. Other times his thoughts wandered. He thought about his mother, who had died when he was a young boy. He remembered some of the songs she had taught him. He thought about his father, who had been so faithful in teaching him about the Lord. His conscience stung when he remembered his father's tears. He had treated his father rudely, and had said some cruel things. He cringed when he thought that he could never ask him for forgiveness.

Once, he brought his father's Bible with him to his room. He remembered how his father had loved to read it, and when he was too tired to read, he would keep it close beside him. Gently, John stroked the Bible's worn cover, but did not want to read it for himself. There were times when John tried to push away the pangs of conscience. Did he really want to give up his friends and his lifestyle to become one of those religious people like his father had been? True, he wasn't enjoying himself lately like he had before his father's death. He'd been telling his friends that he needed time alone, that he missed his father. His friends didn't understand, and told him he should be glad he was rid of "the nagging old man." John resented the way they spoke of his father, and it bothered him that his friends didn't seem to miss him. They called on him less and less often.

John began to look forward to the hour alone in his room. He started to read in his father's Bible, noting with interest the comments written in the

margins. The more John became unhappy with himself, the dearer the Bible became. Shame and guilt
led him to cry out for forgiveness. He could hardly
believe that the Lord would have mercy on him, for
he had ignored and despised his father's pleadings.
Thankfully, the worse John felt about himself, the
more he turned to God's Word, and the more he
cried out for mercy. The Holy Spirit showed him the
beauty of the Savior, and there, finally, John found
the peace and joy his father had always told him
about. For the rest of his life, John kept his promise
to his father, and spent an hour alone in his room—
with God.

—40—
Protection Through Prayer

Verily I say unto you, Whosoever shall not receive the kingdom of God as a little child, he shall not enter therein.

—Mark 10:15

The still form of a little boy lay in the coffin, surrounded by mourning family and friends. A stranger entered the room, and with tears streaming down his face, paused at the coffin to gaze at the boy. He turned and spoke to the little boy's grieving parents.

"You don't know me," he said, "but your boy was a messenger of God to me. One time I was coming down a long ladder from a very high roof, and saw your little boy standing close beside me when I reached the ground. He looked into my face with childish wonder, and asked, 'Weren't you afraid of falling when you were up so high?' And, before I had time to answer, he said, 'Oh, I know why you weren't afraid! You asked God to protect you before you went to work this morning!' I had not prayed; but after that, I never forgot to pray from that day until today, and by God's grace, I will never stop praying until I meet your son in heaven."

—41—
The Sleepless Night

The LORD is nigh unto them that are of a broken heart;
and saveth such as be of a contrite spirit.
—Psalm 34:18

"I wish the clock wouldn't tick so loudly!" muttered Ruth. "I don't know why I can't sleep!"

She tossed and turned in her bed, doubling up her pillow one moment to make it higher, then throwing it aside, trying to find a comfortable position. "I did not steal; I didn't do anything wrong!" she said to herself.

Usually she fell asleep soon after lying down, and slept so soundly that it seemed to her that the night only lasted a few minutes. This time, however, she had listened to the footsteps of her brothers and sisters as they went to their rooms, had heard her father wind up the old clock in the hall, and her mother's voice hushing the baby. All was still now in the house, except the ever-ticking clock, and yet she could not sleep.

Shall I tell you what troubled Ruth, so that the normally comforting sound of the old clock now bothered her so much? Ruth had committed a sin. The little boy who sat next to her in school had a couple of new storybooks which he refused to show her. She had caught glimpses of the colorful covers when he opened his desk, but when she asked again and again if she could please look at the books, Matthew said, "No!"

Ruth wondered what the stories were about and what the pictures looked like. Why did Matthew have to be so selfish? She thought about it so much that she broke the tenth commandment, and coveted: she wished to have Matthew's books for herself.

After the children had gone home, the teacher had locked the schoolhouse door, and left for home. Ruth lingered behind, talking with Katie Waters, a lively, cheerful girl who was afraid of nothing. Ruth had an idea. She asked Katie to climb in the back window with her.

"Sure, I'll do that," answered Katie casually, "but why do you want to do that?"

"I'll show you when we get in," replied Ruth.

Raising the window with little difficulty, she helped Katie climb in. Then she scrambled in after Katie. Ruth led the way to Matthew's desk.

"Look," she said, pointing to the beautiful books. "I want one of those. Matthew wouldn't let me look at them today. I don't know why he brings them to school if he doesn't let anyone else look at them," pouted Ruth.

Katie frowned.

"If you take one, Katie, and give it to me, then we can both say we didn't do it, when the teacher finds out and makes a fuss about it," prodded Ruth.

Katie looked at the books. They were beautiful hardbound children's books, with brightly colored pictures. "Ruth, if you had only wanted to play a trick on Matthew, and just hide one for a while, I'd do it, but stealing is another thing. I don't steal."

"But who would find out, Katie? We could hide it in our barn, and we could read in it every day after school. Matthew is so selfish, he doesn't deserve to have the books!" Ruth added angrily.

"Don't you know, Ruth?" whispered Katie. "God will know it. I'm not taking those books. I'm getting out of here."

Ruth shut the desk, after giving the books another longing look. Katie quickly climbed out of the window, and Ruth caught up to her as she left for home. "Please, Katie, don't tell anyone, ever, about this!" Ruth pleaded.

"Of course not," promised Katie. "I won't tell a soul. I won't even think about it again."

Ruth could not say the same. She thought about

it all the rest of the day. "I don't see why I feel so bad about it," thought Ruth. "I didn't steal. I didn't do anything wrong. Matthew's books are still safely in his desk."

Now, in the darkness, listening to the ticking of the old familiar clock, Ruth did not feel as though she were innocent. What was she supposed to do? She thought that she should ask God to forgive her, but that would mean admitting she had sinned. "No, no!" she thought, "I didn't steal!"

But as the night dragged on, and Ruth became more agitated and nervous, she began to cry. She was guilty; deep down she knew it. Suddenly she remembered a text she had heard recently, "For as he thinketh in his heart, so is he"(Proverbs 23:7a). God saw her heart, and in His eyes, she was a thief. Not only was she a thief, but she had coveted, and then had tried to make her friend a thief, too. No wonder she could find no rest! She knew that only by asking forgiveness could she find rest.

She got out of bed and knelt down. "God, I'm so sorry," she began. Then the whole story came pouring out, along with tears and sobs. Wiping her tears away, she climbed back into bed, and with a deep sigh, drifted off into a sweet sleep.

God looks deeper than our outward behavior. We cannot convince God that keeping His commandments outwardly means that we are without sin. "As he thinketh in his heart, so is he" means

that because we have sin in our hearts, we are con-
demned before God. We need our hearts renewed
in order to please God. Confess your sin and guilt
before Him, and He will make you clean. "Purge me
with hyssop, and I shall be clean: wash me, and I
shall be whiter than snow" (Psalm 51:7).

—42—
The Story of Emilia

Then shall ye call upon me, and ye shall go and pray unto me, and I will hearken unto you. And ye shall seek me, and find me, when ye shall search for me with all your heart. And I will be found of you, saith the LORD.

—Jeremiah 29:12-14a

I want to tell you the true story of a little girl named Emilia. Her parents were godly people who taught Emilia by words and example what a blessed thing it is to be a Christian. Emilia thought often about what she heard, and longed to become one of God's children. One morning, when she was only six years old, her anxiety became so great that she went to her mother to talk about her soul. She cried, and said over and over, "I want Jesus to forgive me. I'm sorry I ever sinned against Him. He has always been so good to me. I'm sorry that I've sometimes argued with my little sister."

Emilia's mother told her once again about the blessed Savior, who is able and willing to save all who repent of their sins, and give themselves to Him. But Emilia's distress continued. Day after day, she would come to her mother in tears because of her sins. Once she said, "What a wicked sinner I am! I want to belong to Jesus. But Christ sees me, and He knows I want to be His child."

Another day, she said, "The anger of God is terrible. I long to be in Jesus' arms, and my heart is full of sorrow because I am not a Christian." She then knelt and prayed with her mother, and afterward said, "What shall I do? I feel so awful! My crying will do me no good."

Emilia kept thinking that if she had come to Christ long before, then He would have received her, but now she said she had lived to be six years old already, and not given her heart to Jesus all that time when He had been so ready to love her and forgive her. It seemed to her that such great ingratitude might never be forgiven. In her prayers, she would repeat many of the Bible promises, such as, "Suffer little children, and forbid them not, to come unto me: for of such is the kingdom of heaven" (Matthew 19:14).

Emilia would pray very often during the day, for she said she wanted to tell God how she felt. She felt that she was a very great sinner, and she wondered if Jesus would forgive her, because she was so wicked. People might have been surprised at this, for she was considered a "good little girl." She was afraid to lie or to disobey her parents; she was kind and polite. Yet, she felt that her heart was dreadfully wicked, because she had not loved God. This was her burden.

She liked to go off alone to pray. "Lord Jesus, help me not to listen to Satan, who wants to destroy my soul. Help me to listen to Thee. Thou hast promised, 'Those that seek me early shall find me' (Proverbs 8: 17b). Fill my heart with Thy love."

Emilia was alone praying by herself one day, when she was able to give her heart to the Lord Jesus Christ. Such light and comfort came into her heart that she could not describe it. She jumped around the room, clapping her little hands for joy. She always remembered the very spot in the living room where she was kneeling. As she grew, she discovered more and more what a dear precious Savior and loving friend Christ is. She learned that even though she was a sinner, the Lord never tired of blessing

her. She gladly served Him all her life, and was a
great blessing to many people, young and old.

Children, do you love the Lord Jesus Christ? If
not, you remain in great danger! Flee to Christ, as
little Emilia did. This little girl was not disappointed, and you won't be either when you go to
Him. "Now therefore hearken unto me, O ye children: for blessed are they that keep my ways"
(Proverbs 8:32).

—43—
The Saints' Everlasting Rest

Set your affection on things above, not on things on the earth.
—Colossians 3:2

Helen sat tucked cozily between her grandfather and grandmother, riding along in their old car. Her glowing face looked young and fresh compared to the wrinkles and silver hair of the dear old people. The cares and sins of seventy years had etched their sorrows on the aged faces of her grandparents. They had not carried their burdens alone, however. They had found the "green pastures" and "still waters" David spoke of in Psalm 23. Helen sat quietly, listening to their conversation, not because she was afraid to talk, but because she loved to hear them speak. Even at her young age, she realized that most likely her beloved grandparents would be in their graves before she reached adulthood.

The dashboard blocked Helen's view in front, and the side windows offered only the tops of trees or buildings for her to see, but she didn't mind.

Whenever she visited her grandparents, she felt

like young Samuel living in the temple with Eli. It was not at all like her own home, where no one found Christ precious, or treasured God's Word. Every summer, however, Helen was permitted to spend several happy weeks at the country home of her mother's parents, and to her it seemed like the very gate of heaven.

Today was a special day: it was Helen's tenth birthday, so this was a special outing. Slowly the car followed the road into the nearby town. When Helen saw the church spire through the side window, she knew they had almost reached their destination. Grandfather carefully guided the old car into a parking space in front of a bookshop. He helped Grandmother and Helen from the car. The bell jingled merrily as they opened the door.

After a pleasant exchange of greetings, Helen heard her grandfather ask the shopkeeper if he had any books suitable for a girl who had just turned ten years old. Her heart fluttered with joy, especially when she saw rows of brightly colored books, filled with fairy tales and stories of fascinating adventures. The owner chose several of the most colorful books and showed them to Grandfather. Helen caught glimpses of the beautiful pictures as he examined the books. With the impatience of her young years, Helen could hardly wait for his decision. But she felt confident that he would choose the best children's book. Grandmother patiently seated herself in one of the chairs provided for customers, while Helen paced up and down the aisle.

"These are not very wise books, I think," said Grandfather at last. "I cannot give my granddaughter these trivial books. Bunyan[1] and Doddridge[2] never wrote such books."

Poor Helen looked dismayed and tears filled her eyes when her grandfather turned away from the attractive books and began to search among the heavy, somber-looking books in the adults' section. At last the old man chose the very darkest and most unattractive book and paid for it. It was wrapped in plain brown paper. The homeward ride was as gloomy for Helen as the ride into town had been pleasant.

When they arrived home, Grandmother made tea, and the book was solemnly presented to Helen. Grandfather urged her to read it carefully and said they prayed it would be blessed to her soul. On the first page, her name was written in clear letters, along with the date. Helen tried to look pleased, but her face clouded over when she read, *The Saints' Everlasting Rest,* by Richard Baxter. The kind, sympathizing grandmother understood the shadow, and prayed in her heart that it might some day prove a comfort for this dear child. The type was very large and distinct, evidently designed for old people. Helen carried it away to her room, having promised rather hesitatingly that she would read it. How sweet were the contents to Helen's grandparents! They did not realize that the thought of eternal rest and joy had not yet entered the thoughts of this active child just setting out on the journey of life. To them the book was precious. To Helen it seemed dingy and boring. She looked at it once, but found the words hard to understand, so she packed it in her suitcase and forgot about it.

Two stones in a churchyard had become mossy with age before this book was needed. The old grandparents had been at rest for many years already. Helen's life had been unusually difficult. At last, during a long illness, she discovered the neglected book. When she read the inscription on the front page, she remembered her promise to her grandparents. She had gray hairs herself now; it was time for her to consider the saints' everlasting rest. Thus the birthday gift became a source of blessed comfort and promise to her weary soul. It reminded her vividly of her beloved grandparents' quiet strength and joy in their dear Lord. Diligently, earnestly, Helen read the old book. The print was not too large now for her dimmed eyes; the thought of rest was welcome indeed; she no longer considered the old book boring.

In the end, Grandfather's choice had been a wise one. Long after a colorful storybook would have lost its appeal, this gloomy-looking volume kept its value. The old Puritan author's words were like "apples of gold in pictures of silver" (Proverbs

25:11b). They directed Helen to the Lord Jesus Christ and the Word of God. Along with the Bible, this book became like a dear friend to Helen. The binding was worn, the margins penciled, and the pages dog-eared when Helen read it for the last time, and finally entered into the saints' everlasting rest with her beloved grandparents to meet her dear Savior in glory.

---

[1]John Bunyan (1628-1688) was an English Puritan writer and preacher. He was imprisoned for twelve years for preaching illegally. While in prison he wrote the famous book, *The Pilgrim's Progress*.

[2]Phillip Doddridge (1702-1751) was a "non-conformist" or "Dissenter," which meant that he did not agree with all the doctrines taught by the Church of England. He founded a school in 1730 which trained several godly men for the ministry. His best known work is *The Rise and Progress of Religion in the Soul*. He also wrote several hymns.

—44—
An Attentive Daughter

How forcible are right words!
—Job 6:25a

There was once a town in America which the Lord blessed with a revival. Many people who normally had no interest in religion began attending church services and prayer meetings regularly. The Holy Spirit worked saving grace in the hearts of many people. One evening, Mrs. Angus and her little daughter, Sarah, attended a meeting. The minister was speaking on the importance of family worship, and the dangers of neglecting this duty. Sarah listened attentively. She was trying to understand what the minister was talking about. What was family worship? Sadly, Sarah's family had never taken the time for Bible reading and prayer.

Sarah looked up at her mother, who was also listening with interest. She tugged on her mother's sleeve. "Mama," she whispered, "is the minister talking to you?"

These words pierced Mrs. Angus's heart like an arrow. The Holy Spirit used Sarah's question to convict Mrs. Angus of this sin of neglecting such an important duty. A change came about in the Angus family. Church attendance, family worship, Christian books, Bible study all became things to be treasured and loved. Are these things important to you and your family?

—45—
A Woman Set Free

Neither is there salvation in any other: for there is none other name under heaven given among men, whereby we must be saved.

—Acts 4:12

Around the time of the Reformation, a woman, whom we will name Mary, was troubled by her sins, and had tried her best to do what the Roman Catholic Church taught. She dutifully made confession[1] to her priest, and carefully carried out the payment for sin that the priest required of her. She could find no relief, however, in these rituals. She was also disgusted with the world, troubled that people sinned so lightly and seemed to think all was well if only a priest told them so.

In desperation, Mary decided to enter a convent.[2] She believed that this would calm her troubled conscience. How blissful, she thought, to live a life of uninterrupted piety! She would pray seven times a day, and confess her sins as often as she could. There would be no earthly matters to distract her from being holy. It would be the nearest thing to heaven. She would be the best nun that ever lived, she thought. But her happiness did not last. She dis-

covered that her conscience found no relief in endless prayers, confessions, and acts of contrition. The harder she tried, the worse she felt, and no one seemed to understand her. They shook their heads and told her not to worry, and counseled her to pray the rosary[3] an extra time, or do a good deed for the poor or the sick. To her dismay, she found that the nuns were not as pious as she had thought they would be. Although they took their vows seriously, they only went through the motions required of them. Though they followed the rules exactly, there was no joy, no love. Mary was more miserable than ever, and made up her mind to leave the convent.

Next, Mary tried to find relief in pilgrimages.[4] She made two trips to Switzerland, to pray and worship at holy sites, but nothing seemed to help. Her conscience would not be silenced. She asked her priest to help her. What could appease the longings of her heart? Her priest could not help her. In a scornful tone, he asked her, "Are you saying that the traditions and rituals of the church were not good enough for you?"

"I don't mean that sir!" exclaimed Mary. "It's just that I cannot find peace."

"Thousands before you have found peace in the holy traditions of our blessed church. Do you think you are better than all those other people? Does God have to do something special just for you?"

"No, no!" wept Mary, feeling worse than ever. "Just tell me what I must do to atone for my wickedness!"

Poor Mary! She did not know what the Bible taught. She had never heard the gospel, the good news of Jesus Christ. But God knew all about her. He knew her struggles, for the Holy Spirit Himself had worked them in her. He would not leave her now; He would show her the true Way of salvation.

One day, Mary heard about a priest named Martin Boos.[5] Some people said this priest had strange ideas, and that he did not agree with everything the church taught. Mary began to wonder if this man might understand her. Could it be that he wrestled with the same questions Mary did? Could it be that he had found the answer? Would he even be willing to speak to her? She hardly dared to hope—she had been disappointed so many times before.

Martin Boos lived near Mary's town, and, to her delight, the priest was willing to speak to her. He was very kind, and Mary's nervousness eased a bit. What was more, he understood her! At last, someone understood! And he knew the solution! Eagerly, Mary listened, soaking up every word. She knew, without a doubt, that this was the answer! The godly priest told her about Jesus Christ, who came to die for the sins of His people. Only Jesus can forgive sin, he explained. That is why Mary would never find rest in anything apart from the Savior. At last, Mary found what her soul had been seeking. In Christ, she found the rest and comfort which He offers to the weary and heavy laden. She was so happy!

From that time, however, Mary found no delight in her rosary, and other rituals of the church. This troubled her, and she wondered if God was angry with her for not feeling any love for these things. She returned to Martin Boos.

"What is it that occupies your time, Mary? Why do you not wish to use your rosary and go to the confessional anymore?" Boos asked.

"I can do nothing but love Jesus, because He is in me and with me!" she cried. "Nothing brings joy to my heart, but thoughts of Him! When I say the prayers to Mary, I feel uneasy and sad."

Martin Boos smiled kindly. "It is no heresy to love Jesus and think of Him. To do everything out of love to Him is of more worth than many rosaries."

Mary felt relieved. But soon Satan began to whisper in her heart that Martin Boos was not a good priest. After all, he did not agree with many things the Roman Catholic Church taught. Many people suspected him of being a heretic. How could she trust him? He could not be worth much, Satan told her, if he did not value rosaries. Mary did not want to tell her new friend these thoughts, but she became so uneasy, that at last she made the fifteen-mile trip to Martin Boos, and told him what was bothering her.

To her amazement, he laughed heartily! "You are right, Mary! In myself I am of no worth at all! But remember this: what I have taught you is of infinite value, for it was taught by Jesus Christ Himself. Continue in the faith, Mary, and do not be discouraged!"

Some weeks later, a feast of indulgences[6] was held in her neighborhood. Mary did not want to attend; she did not want to be anywhere near such deceit. Instead, she traveled once again to visit Martin Boos. She told him she wanted nothing to do with indulgences. When he asked her why not, she answered, "Jesus is my absolution,[7] since He died for me. His blood alone is the absolution for all my sins."

"Who is teaching you this?" asked Boos, impressed by her certainty.

"No one," Mary replied. "The thought comes by itself into my mind. Jesus takes away my sins. He has taken away everything else with which I tried to save myself. I found no comfort in confessing my sins to a priest; I found no relief in the convent or by using the rosary or making pilgrimages. They gave me neither rest nor peace. I am now convinced that only the blood of Jesus takes away my sins."

Mary did not fully realize that it was the Holy Spirit who taught her. In the time in which Mary lived, the Bible was a rare Book. Few people knew and believed what it taught. People like Martin Boos were as shining lights on a hill who taught seeking, restless souls about the Lord Jesus Christ. The Holy Spirit had not let Mary rest until she found salvation in the blood of the Lamb of God.

Mary never owned a Bible, and perhaps never even saw one during her entire life. Yet, she was God's child, saved by the atoning blood of Jesus Christ. Will Mary enter the kingdom of God, and shall we, who know so much more of the Bible than she did, be sent into everlasting darkness? Do not rest, dear children, until you know, just like Mary did, the joy of being forgiven by the Lord Jesus Christ.

---

[1]Roman Catholic people are taught to make confession of their sins regularly to their priest. The priest sits in a little booth, and is separated from the people by a veil, so they cannot see each other. The

priest decides on the appropriate punishment and then grants absolution, which means that he tells them their sins are forgiven.

²A convent is a home for nuns who live within its walls. They dedi-
cate themselves to a life of Roman Catholic piety.

³A rosary is a string of beads to help the person count his prayers.
Each bead represents a special set of prayers to the Virgin Mary.

⁴Pilgrimages were journeys people made to places declared sacred by
the Roman Catholic Church.

⁵Martin Boos (1762-1825), a German Roman Catholic theologian, was
born at Huttenried in Bavaria on December 25, 1762. Orphaned at the
age of four, he was reared by an uncle at Augsburg, who finally sent him
to the University of Dillingen. There he laid the foundation of the mod-
est piety by which his whole life was distinguished. After serving as
priest in several Bavarian towns, he made his way in 1799 to Linz in
Austria, where he was welcomed by Bishop Gall, and set to work first
at Leonding and then at Waldneukirchen, becoming pastor at Gall-
neukirchen in 1806. His pietistic movement won considerable follow-
ers among the Roman Catholic laity, and even attracted some fifty or
sixty priests. The death of Gall and other powerful friends, however,
exposed him to bitter enmity and persecution from about 1812, and he
had to answer endless accusations in the consistorial courts. His enemies followed him when he returned to Bavaria, but in 1817 the Pruss-
ian government appointed him to a professorship at Düsseldorf, and in
1819 gave him the pastorate at Sayn near Neuwied. He died on the 29th
of August, 1825. (From www.1911encyclopedia.org.)

⁶Indulgences were certificates that people could buy, which stated
that the person's sins—past, present, and future—were forgiven.

⁷Absolution means payment for sin.